Time Invades
the Cathedral

Time Invades the Cathedral

TENSIONS IN THE SCHOOL OF HOPE

by

WALTER H. CAPPS

FORTRESS PRESS

Philadelphia

Library of Congress Catalog Card Number 77–171496

ISBN 0–8006–0106–8

2999H71   Printed in the United States of America   1–106

To the Sisters of the Immaculate Heart Community, creative mediators of the future's religious tensions, for whom this study was originally prepared

Stones sleep, plants dream, animals toss in their dreams as though they wanted to wake up, and man awakes. A great illumination—a great awakening—goes through the world! Time invades the cathedral! Horizontal succession is joined to the vertical hierarchy of the real.

—Ernst Bloch

Contents

Foreword

Books and dissertations on the theology of hope have recently been appearing in mounting number. Some of them are so insightful that they actually contribute to the movement's advance; others almost stifle the whole enterprise. I myself have often felt uneasy about being made the subject of a book, because I know that I have only made a beginning and am not yet ready to wrap matters up. The things others set down in writing about me seem to fix with almost unacceptable finality thoughts which are still very much in flux. It is almost as if an exploratory operation were to be abruptly stopped just as it was getting under way.

In this respect Walter Capps has done something quite different. I read his manuscript from beginning to end at a single sitting. Learning from it all the while and enjoying it more and more as I went along, I could not put it down. It not only provides clear and reliable information about Ernst Bloch, Johannes Baptist Metz, and myself; it also makes its own independent contribution to the theology of hope and its ongoing quest. Capps does not just observe the flow of philosophical and theological discussion from a safe vantage point, high and dry on a shaded bank; he plunges right into the river with us to do some swimming of his own. As a result, he is able to discern with greater clarity the strengths and weaknesses of the movement, where it makes significant advances and where it goes astray. It was never my wish to develop a following of worshipful hangers-on who would faithfully imitate me. We in Germany, at least, have had more than our fill of such theological "schools" and sects. *Das Prinzip Hoffnung* is no philosophical system, and the theology of hope is no *Summa Theologica*. Each is simply a critical stance, a polemical position, a controverted direction, taken within the conflicts of our time. Their purpose is to effect change: changes in consciousness and in our personal and political situation. To that end what is needed is not devoted disciples but close comrades, companions who from their own perspective and presuppositions will catch a glimpse and actually enter into the future of which we speak. Walter Capps is just such a man, an independent and critical traveler along the common path.

Theology is not the abstract business of a small esoteric band of recluses. A theology worthy of the name actually attempts to exercise a healing function in church, society, and culture. Its quest is not for some ultimate formulation that will be forever "right," but only for that liberating word for today which can set free men who are inwardly and outwardly oppressed. This is something Capps has grasped very well, and I have the feeling that his finger is really on the pulse of our time.

The cathedrals of the Middle Ages are splendid structures. We think of them as marvels of human achievement, complete and perfect in every way—and so they are. In many cases, however, their construction required several centuries of continuing effort. They were usually regarded by the men of their day as unfinished. Indeed, according to one old legend, the cathedrals could never be brought to final completion until the Last Day. Each succeeding generation was to carry the work further. There was a kind of horizontal eschatology about them. The same is true also of the great theological systems of past eras. To be sure, when the masters brought together all that was known to the men of their time they were essaying to present the fullness of the wisdom of God, but from Thomas Aquinas to Karl Barth they were well aware that all our knowledge is "imperfect" and that, as Paul said, we shall "know fully" only in God's future.

There are times for cathedrals and theological summations, but there are also times for tents—for moving out and traveling lightly. There are times in which a whole epoch finds its consummation, but there are also times of transition. Paul left no manual of theology, only some letters to certain struggling congregations. Luther wrote no dogmatics, only some treatises aimed at reforming the current situation in church and society. It was only *after* Paul that in the early church there developed the great systems of theology. It was only *after* Luther that there appeared the early Protestant dogmatics.

The time in which we live, it seems to me, is not one in which an epoch is coming to fulfillment. It is not a time for cathedrals and massive theologies. Ours is a time of rapid transition in every area of life, and nobody knows just where the changes are taking us. For many inquiring—and protesting—Christians, ours is a time to head for the wilderness— or the catacombs. Ought not theology too, therefore, to try to move out from the massive cathedrals of its distinguished traditions in order to bring the spirit of hope and the remembrance of the cross into the midst of these tumultuous changes? But to move in that direction is necessarily to adopt a critical and liberating style of writing. The theologians of hope know perfectly well that their theology is at best a passageway, a bridge, a transitional stage, possibly even a tiny light on the path from exodus to the promised land. They do not presume to think that what they are saying is all that needs to be said. Their theology—to use an analogy—may give the soup its savor, but it is not the whole broth. Their emphasis on hope must therefore remain open to fresh evaluations of remembrance. Their political theology, while intended as an antidote against pious withdrawal into the private life of the believer, does not mean to exclude the indispensable personal dimension which belongs to faith itself. Their activism is directed against apathy, both religious and secular, but not against joy in living, adoration, meditation, and ascetic ways of life. Hence there are bound to be further surprises in store as this particular theological style continues to take new turns. Capps makes some perceptive suggestions along this line.

I should like to close with a brief personal note. Ernst Bloch's *Das Prinzip Hoffnung* has, of course, made a deep impression on me and I am greatly indebted to its author for many insights. But the theology of hope was in my thoughts —and writings—long before that. After all, studying under Hans-Joachim Iwand, Ernst Käsemann, and Arnold van Ruler was bound to have an effect on me. One cannot judge a theologian exclusively in terms of his mentors, but neither should one judge him wholly in terms of his philosophical expression. While that is important too, it is a relatively incidental matter.

A real theologian is like Jacob wrestling the angel at the Jabbok. Rilke put it this way:

> How small, that with which we wrestle,
>
> But how great, that which wrestles with us.

It always seems to me as if the theme and subject matter with which theology has to do is "that which wrestles with us," and that we theologians are like Jacob: we emerge from the struggle beaten and limping. That is why our best theology is "imperfect," shattered by that Greater One. And that is why theology is at best only a directional indicator, pointing to the mysterious God who draws us to him, drives us on, and continually eludes all our concepts, images, and symbols.

Deus semper major!

JÜRGEN MOLTMANN

Tübingen
September, 1971

Preface

In another place, at an earlier time, under different auspices, I wrote an essay in which I attempted to preview the promise of the hope orientations of Ernst Bloch, Jürgen Moltmann, and Johannes Metz.[1] That essay was largely anticipatory. It was also self-consciously premature, having been prepared well in advance of the fuller expression of many of the contentions which lay within the hope school. At that time I argued that the movement seemed to exhibit unusual promise by virtue of its ability to make religious and philosophical proposals in strikingly novel ways. But, as I have indicated, my argument was registered some time ago, before the hope movement could have been known and understood very surely. The earlier essay was also descriptive. It made no attempt to provide detailed analyses of the thoughts of those most closely associated with the school. Nor did I try to trace the historical backgrounds out of which the contentions of the school have come. Instead, I simply contented myself with morphological portrayal. My purpose was to locate the hope school, and to treat it within a framework in which it could also

1. The study was originally published in a special issue of *Cross Currents* 18, no. 3 (1968), then in revised and expanded form as "Mapping the Hope Movement," in *The Future of Hope,* ed. Walter H. Capps (Philadelphia: Fortress Press, 1970).

gain recognition. I undertook this, I recognized even then, before any but a few people had had time to try the school on for size.

In the meantime, the hope school has developed. It has matured and changed. Some say it has already run its course, and that its early promise has been spent. Whether that be the case or not, it seems both appropriate and necessary now to test the occurrence of the hope movement in detail. Sufficient time has passed to justify a fuller description of the hope movement than was possible before; and the perspectives are available to enable one to approach an assessment of the school with methodological confidence. Futhermore, the contentions of the hope thinkers are consistent enough to be readily understood, and important enough to deserve a hearing.

In assessing the promise of hope theology, my purpose is also to provide a kind of primer on the subject. I do not intend to give an exhaustive account, but instead to suggest some useful perspectives. The substance of the study is supplied by the writings of the three principal spokesmen within the movement—Ernst Bloch, the philosophical catalyst; Jürgen Moltmann, the primary Protestant theologian; and Johannes B. Metz, the Catholic religio-political theorist. I shall understand the "hope school" to be the product of the insights of these three figures. Following a current convention, I am treating them as though they are members of a team which champions a single cause. They do share common interests, of course, and their proposals often sound very much alike. I recognize too, however, that each of them comes to proposals about hope from varying backgrounds, with different sets of purposes, and by paths which do not always traverse a common terrain. They will be treated here together, despite the fact that variations between them are sometimes greater than areas of agreement. I recognize both factors, and will save a comparison and contrast of their views for a later chapter.

In previewing my approach to the subject, I must also say something about the perspective from which this book is written. As will be obvious to readers who know something of my background, my study reflects a deliberate attitudinal tone. To account for this attitude, if the reader is interested in the matter, I can simply cite autobiographical factors, without necessarily giving an apology. Like many others trained in the histories of theology and philosophy, I suppose, I can recall the great excitement which accompanied my first experience in grappling with a comprehensive system of thought. Perhaps because of my Lutheran background, a training which carried suspicions toward as well as appreciation for systematic ways of thinking, it was not until I encountered the philosophy of Alfred North Whitehead in an undergraduate course in philosophy that I found the integrative power of a systematic pattern of reflection compelling. Once I had gotten hold of its basic components, I was confident that I could begin at any point in Whitehead's great system and think my way through all of it. I eventually came to use Whitehead's system as the framework by which I understood everything. I employed Whiteheadian categories in making ethical decisions, arranging what I knew of intellectual history, undergirding my religious aspirations, and even in designing a vocation. The more I employed the system the more obvious was its utility. It harmonized those things which had been disparate before, and provided me with insights that I had not had before. In addition, it gave me intellectual confidence. For the first time, perhaps, I felt that my attitude to life was harmonious with life, and that it could be defended. I was sure that I had been given the key which unlocked the overarching schematic puzzles.

As Lord Byron put it, "A cask always retains a hint of the first wine it took in." And that has been my experience, for, to this day, I have not been able to leave Whitehead's system of thought behind, even though I have come to understand it in different terms. But, predictably, I have moved from the innocence of that first apprehension of systematic harmony to the "worldly wisdom" of having had the same kind of experience on a succession of other occasions. Each time, I suppose, the experience becomes more predictable and, in turn, less compelling and satisfying; and yet it remains impressive and thoroughly authentic. In short, I have discovered that the fruits from insight into Whitehead's system could also be plucked from a number of other trees of systematic reflection. What had happened under Whiteheadian stimulation could have occurred under Thomistic or even Hegelian auspices, perhaps, just as well; and it might have come faster had I read Paul Tillich earlier or become acquainted with Neoplatonic writings. Once I had embarked on the quest toward putting all things together neatly, there was virtually no end to my lusting after order until I had done just that. But the difficulty came when I recognized that the thrill of systematic closure could be produced by any one of a number of meaningful schemes or structural sets, and that selection between them was always somewhat arbitrary. At last, standing back to observe my apparent perpetual fickleness, I gained insight into the logic of conceptual thinking itself. Then, instead of greeting each new system I encountered, whether theological or philosophical, as though it were a potential marriage partner (to whom I would have to give myself in some unqualified way), I came to see them as representing a certain genus of reflection of which there were various species. Instead of approaching each one as a would-be devotee, I came to look for the techniques they employed and gave myself to analyses of their conceptual strengths and weaknesses. And, from that time on, my approach to theological systems has been cautious, analytical, and, I believe, disciplined. I see them not as surrogates of either the religious or the reflective life, but as more or less resourceful but partial ways of giving expression to both.

Hence, when I came in touch with the so-called theology of hope, I came as one who did not expect it to be able to be all things. The hope school could not become as Whitehead's philosophy once was for me, for that kind of preciousness cannot be revived. Furthermore, I did not want the school to become more than it was. I expected that it would have conceptual strengths and weaknesses, but I did not ask that it correctly summarize either the Christian faith or philosophical truth. My interests were infinitely more modest. I was looking first for something that might be fresh and engaging, even novel and innovative. It had to be instructive, and it was required to sustain my initial intrigue. If it manifested itself as being agile and full of delights, I knew I could also assess its ability to portray truth.

Hearing this confession, some readers will think me disillusioned with theological reflection. Advocates of the hope position will surely be disappointed with my portrayal, and will point to my "confession" as an indication that my interpretation of their cause should not be taken with utmost seriousness. My response is simply that I understand patterns of theology to be more like works of art than summaries of truth, recognizing all the while that works of art can also be indicators of truth. I am interested in what such patterns portray, but I am probably more interested in the designs they employ to portray it. The skill I seek to develop, then, is not that of testing affirmations to decide whether or not I can accept them. Such exercises are useful, of course, and go on continually. Obviously, there is no point in trying forever to bracket them out; and much is to be gained by doing them well. But that is not the program on which I have embarked here. Instead, the specific skill I seek both to foster and illustrate has to do with the more dispassionate analytical work of separating out the kinds of ingredients which become party to systematic reflection. And, because the distinction quickly turns into a stress, I am probably more interested in form than content. At least, I approach content via trained sensitivity to form. In sum, I am approaching the hope ideo-schemes of Bloch, Moltmann, and Metz with a controlling interest in their conceptual mechanics, for I am sure that much of the material of the stance lies implicit in its particular propensity for form.

Thus, I have taken special note of the primary images which the hope thinkers seek to articulate, the schematic factors which they employ, and the kinds of diagrammatic sketches by means of which they offer illustrations. It is interesting to me, for example, that the underlying conceptual scheme used by the hope school thinkers runs horizontally rather than vertically, isolates the future tense rather than the present or the past, and gives higher priority to social than to individual concerns. It also intrigues me that the dominant thrust of the position is pointed to the formation of a new human community. That seems to be its final intention; everything else within the system plays a supportive role. Other theological stances seem to want to help the self discover the self. Some others try to locate or refurbish transcendence. But the hope school is interested in community. It wants to underscore the conditions for the ideal community. Thus, because its stress is on achieving ideal relationships between persons, the pattern is not as well able to relate to individual subjective matters. In theological terms, the hope school can give articulation to the concept of "the kingdom of God," but finds itself somewhat embarrassed when called upon to talk about "beatitude." It can draw upon its horizontal projection to speak meaningfully about man's future destiny, but it can say very little by way of supporting those institutions—church and state, to name but two of them—which tend to require vertical hierarchization. But, as I have come to know it, this is the way it is with conceptual patterns. One cannot expect more of them than he has a right to expect. They can affirm some things, and some of those things well, but usually at the expense of other things which someone else should be affirming. And, unless one requires more of conceptual patterns than it is appropriate to require, such inadequacies are not necessarily signs of weakness or oversight. Often they simply mean that their designer has been consistent in the way he has thought things through.

But this is enough for now by way of prefiguring my attitude. I will save for later a discussion of the reasons I have for finding the hope movement disappointing in some respects. And I will postpone for now some suggestions as to how I understand its strengths. In the initial portion of my work I want to return to the map work which I offered in *The Future of Hope.* This time, however, since time has passed, I have chosen to develop some perspectives within which the thought of the three chief spokesmen for the school can be placed. I shall begin with the set of images upon which they frequently draw; then I shall turn to the writings of each of them. Finally, I shall attempt an assessment of their contentions as well as an evaluation of their place in an ongoing discussion of the matters they take up. The first part of the book, the first four chapters, is largely expository; the second part is more analytical, interpretative, and critical. My argument throughout is that the hope thinkers give expression to one of two dominant religious strains within Christianity, which, taken by itself, is partial. But I shall save the detailing of this argument for the proper place in my portrayal of the movement.

The impetus for this book came from some lectures I was invited to give at Immaculate Heart College in Los Angeles in the spring of 1970, and, in different form, at a conference of Lutheran pastors at Asilomar, California later the same year. The hearers in both places were responsive to my suggestions, and provided me with insights, some of which, I trust, I have carried onto these pages. The first stimulus for the book dates back to the early summer of 1966, and to a conversation with my earliest guide in theological conceptual analysis, Professor George A. Lindbeck of Yale University. Though relatively brief, the conversation launched my interest in the hope movement. In the course of exercising that interest, I have also had the privilege of getting to know Professor Jürgen Moltmann of Tübingen University, and am pleased now to count him as a trusted friend. I have prepared this study with these two catalysts of thought in mind. Hinda Elmore in Santa Barbara and Barbara Coysh in Oxford deserve thanks for valuable typing services, and Leah Ann Hallisey for research assistance. Finally, I want to record my thanks to Lois, and to Lisa and Todd, for steady support and interesting diversions both at home and in transit.

ONE

A Formative Image

> But enclosed! That's the trouble: an enclosed world be-
> comes a prison of the spirit. One longs to get out, one longs
> to move. One realises that symmetry and consistency, what-
> ever their merits, are enemies of movement.
>
> —Kenneth Clark

We begin by considering the cathedral.

There was a time, so the analogy begins, when a man could leave his world and enter a cathedral without being conscious of having moved anywhere. The world inside the cathedral was so much like the world outside the cathedral that leaving the one for the other carried no break, shock, nor interruption of the common routine. The world inside mirrored the world outside since both were formed by the same set of aspirations. The regulation of life outside was effected by the same disposition as the regulation of life inside the cathedral. There was inside, and there was outside, but within one and the same circle. A man would go inside from outside through the large doors of the cathedral; remain in there for awhile, then go outside by the same doors through which he had entered the cathedral. He could do this repeatedly, throughout his lifetime. He could expect that his children and his children's children would do the same. It would be inconceivable to him that a situation might develop which would challenge the assumption that inside and outside were simply two spheres within a unified world. For him, for them, there was but one world, not two, not more. The cathedral stood as the focal point of a harmonized world. It was the most prominent structure on the landscape, the veritable apex of the world. Because of the cathedral, the world itself was a kind of parish. Its work and play came under the aegis, and within the light and shadows of the cathedral. It was the treasury house of the great works of art, the prime location for educational activity, the place where plays were performed and music played. Everything religious, social, and cultural eventually pointed to it. Anything which registered anywhere else could find a visible place (and, a kind of active sacramental crowning) within the cathedral. In multiple senses, the cathedral "summarized" the life of the people. Entering the cathedral, a man really had not moved onto new, strange, or different ground.

There was a time, apparently, when this was so. Many men say so, and the analogy provides testimony. But that time, they also say, is no more.

The process of religious and cultural transition, to which allusion has been made, represents one of the fundamental contentions of the hope school. In almost uniform terms, each of the foremost proponents of a hope philosophy— Ernst Bloch, Jürgen Moltmann, Johannes B. Metz, and a host of others—can be understood to be pointing to the process by which the exodus from a cathedral-dominated landscape has occurred. They regard that exodus as both a cultural and a socio-political phenomenon in the Western world. They are talking, of course, about the so-called process of secularization and the inversion it implies with respect to sacred and profane modes of existence. But they are not just trend tracers nor is their prime intention to chronicle what "modern man" is thinking. Their contentions are not derived from representative samplings. Rather, they are concerned about the displacement of cathedral-oriented life by attitudes arranged according to other sets of images. The human alienation which is so obvious to them is also taken as a cultural fact, and is depicted in terms of estrangement from the cathedral. Hence, one can argue that he gets to the heart of the hope contentions quickest of all when he considers their interpretation of the cathedral, and, more specifically, their assessment of the effects of time upon the cathedral's career.

All the members of the hope school have grown up in lands in which cathedrals are very prominent; hence, what time does to the edifice of a cathedral has been visible to them. For all of them, too, the cathedral is not simply qualified by time, but also by the ravages of war. They know too what war can do to delicate religious and cultural fiber. The most direct portrayal of the contrast between the "old" and the "new" in the apprehension of cathedrals is to be found in the writings of Ernst Bloch. In an informal, impromptu address to a group of students, Bloch said:

> Stones sleep, plants dream, animals toss in their dreams as though they wanted to wake up, and man awakes. A great illumination—a great awakening—goes through the world! Time invades the cathedral![1]

Time invades the cathedral! The action implicit in that image forms the driving disposition of the hope movement. It is present also in Jürgen Moltmann's declaration that, following World War II, there could never be a return to the old conditions.

What does it mean, then, to say that time has invaded the cathedral? What can time do to a cathedral? Does it

1. Ernst Bloch, "Man as Possibility," in *The Future of Hope,* ed. Walter H. Capps (Philadelphia: Fortress Press, 1970), p. 56.

simply erode the cathedral's walls? Does it also affect the cathedral's symbolic capacities? Does it spoil its abilities to serve as a center of culture? Or does time alter the world within which the cathedral is set? And, if time can do that too, has it changed the context over which the cathedral had extended itself? Is time real?

And how shall the man of religious sensitivity respond to this metamorphosis? What should his attitude be? Is it an event to be celebrated? Should he rejoice? Should he be sad? Should he long for the bygone day when the evidences of a unified world were visible? Should he look back on that age with nostalgia? Or, should he interpret its passing as a sign of his own recently acquired liberation, a token of the long-awaited success of human courage? Has the world lost its center? Or, has man come of age? Did man come of age when the world lost its center? Or was it merely that the cathedral aged?

And where does the metamorphosis occur? Is it in the "world," that is, on the landscape? Is it at some point "out there"? Or, is it internal—a subjective phenomenon occurring within self-consciousness? In either respect, does the occurrence affect all men, or just some men? If some men only, must those men be members of a religious community —the holy catholic church, for example? Or is it an occurrence in which men participate by virtue of birthright? If a birthright, does it accrue to all men, or some men? If it depends on specific religiously distinguishing characteristics, will it affect all men so distinguished or only some of the more sensitive? Is it also a cultural fact?

The responses to such questions offered by the hope thinkers are introduced by the thesis that time has destroyed the happy correspondence which once existed between the world and the cathedral. Because of change, and the increments of time, one can no longer move from the world into the cathedral, and back again, without being aware of it. To move from the world into the cathedral, and back again, requires a set of adjustments which, for some men, at one time, were not at all necessary.

For the most part, when they also prescribe responses to the situation they have analyzed, the hope thinkers are practitioners of time and change rather than advocates of permanence. They react positively to time; they do not bemoan the passing of permanence. For them, time is not some unkempt, unwelcome intruder, the bearer of nothing but threats and devastation. On the contrary, whatever cathedral there is must be sustained by time if it is to be real at all. Time, then, is not really a destructive force, for it extends, secures, and appropriates.

Of course, the hope thinkers are not simply talking about cathedrals. They are using cathedrals as indications of something else, namely, as the fundamental loci of an earlier integrated symbolic world. Cathedrals are seen as the very fulcra of culture, the eyes through which all of Western civilization has passed. The cathedral is held up because of the function it enjoyed of serving as the center, the veritable apex of the world. The cathedral was preserver, container, and restrainer, all at once; it was both sanctuary and fort. According to the analogy, then, the cathedral stands as the bastion of permanence. It gives permanence to an institution, and secures permanence against the enemy, change and time. As it was conceived, the cathedral owned a stake in Plato's age-old question: "What is it that abides when all else passes away?"[2] The cathedral has reference to the eternal realities, those which abide when everything else

2. This, of course, is a paraphrase of the question raised in Plato's *Timaeus* (27d), "What is that which always is and has no becoming, and what is that which is always becoming and never is?" (Quotation taken from *The Collected Dialogues of Plato*, ed. Edith Hamilton and Huntington Cairns [New York: Bollingen Foundation, 1961], p. 1161.)

passes away. It was designed to serve the eternal realities. Hence, during its regime, the vision of those who worshiped within it was set on those things which would not pass away; and worship itself was designed to root the individual and the community in those values which "passing away" can neither destroy nor diminish.[3]

Those who saw things this way also tended to view God, for example, as the God of permanence, the stabilizer of order, the sustainer of the eternal values (or, in Augustinian language, the container of the eternal forms). Similarly, the world, by contrast, was regarded as a lesser place. The world is that which "passes away." According to the same proportions, the visible things have a lesser status and goodness than the invisible things. Socially, too, this scheme ascribes priority to those offices and occupations which participate most fully and directly in permanence. The tasks which involved greater involvement in change and flux were assumed to be menial and to have lesser importance. Kings, popes, archbishops, and bishops fared well, and civil magistrates were highly positioned. The clergy stood over and above the laity, and the nobles were rated above the servants. Philosophically, too, permanent things were accorded greater value than things that change. Permanent things were conceived as being "up," at the top of the hierarchy, while less permanent things (and things governed by flux and change) were placed at the bottom the vertical plane. But, by means of a hierarchical ordering, everything was linked to everything else. The entire world was under-

3. For illustrative accounts of the pervasiveness of this structural style during the medieval era, see Arthur O. Lovejoy, *The Great Chain of Being* (Cambridge: Harvard University Press, 1936); C. S. Lewis, *The Discarded Image* (London: Cambridge University Press, 1964); and Erwin Panofsky, *Gothic Architecture and Scholasticism* (Cleveland: World Publishing Company, 1957).

stood to be a parish, a unitary field which had been sub-
divided and placed under the control of a simple overarching principle. The contents of the "parish" world, though
many and varied, were arranged in harmony, in propor-
tionate scale. Consequently, when time invades the structure of the cathedral, its presence carries the power of
being able to disorient the original scheme and, perhaps, of
arranging its components in a new pattern of assembly. All
of this, the analogy implies.

What happens, then, when time invades the cathedral?
First, from a structural perspective, a vertical disposition is
challenged by one which runs horizontally almost exclusively. According to the analogy, cathedrals were known
for the facility with which their combined height and depth
trained the eye to move from things transitory to things
transcendent. As designed, they performed an uplifting,
edifying function. And the movement from things transitory
to things transcendent was understood to be in keeping
with the general tendency of things within the world itself.
At the time of its greatest flourishing, the cathedral was
supported intellectually by the principle of *analogia entis*
(the analogy of being) which made it schematically possible to hierarchize virtually every element within human
experience. Construed in analogical terms, the cathedral
was both a skeleton and a blueprint of the world. The
cathedral was the visual symbolization of the very architecture of reality itself. And the general disposition of that
architecture was vertical rather than horizontal, so that
permanence would be instantiated over change.

But when time invades the cathedral, a horizontal force—
a disposition which trains the eye toward things horizontal
and puts process in motion—places vertical projection in
jeopardy. The new disposition does not simply bring the

cathedral down. No, as Ernst Bloch notes, the cathedral remains standing there; vertical hierarchization remains.[4] But something of its very life has been threatened. Its vitality is drained away. It remains, but more and more as a cultural anachronism, a relic of a former time left standing following the devastation wrought by the incursion of the opposite tendency.

This is a classic battle which has been waged for years under various forms. It has been repeated over and over again in the history of Western culture. Indeed, to a certain extent, the history of Western religious thought can be told in terms of the interaction between these two underlying but diverse currents; the one builds upon permanence, and the other gives normative status to time and change. Most Christian theological positions, if they are consistent with themselves, can be depicted according to one or the other of these two styles. The differences between them depend to a large extent on the way they give direction to religious aspiration, or to the place they give to transcendence. As a general rule, when aspirations are directed "skyward" and transcendence is positioned above us, the theological scheme is oriented toward permanence rather than change. But, on the other hand, when the same foci are placed ahead of us, in a future time tense rather than in a plane above us, prominence is given to change and time rather than to permanence. The reason for this deviation is partially obvious. To guide aspirations to a plane above us is to imply that the values are somehow "always there," but in a dimension which is neither common nor public. Values then become eternal in a nontemporal sense. To guide aspirations forward, on the other hand, is to imply that we haven't yet arrived at that point in time in which those

4. Bloch, "Man as Possibility," p. 57.

values have been actualized. They are not "always there," but, more appropriately, they are "not yet." (A contention made both operational and popular in the hope school is that even God is a "still not yet.") And, if ideals are going to be realized or actualized, movement must occur through which the distance between "here" and "there" can be overcome. When the seat of transcendence is located above us, then the conceptual scheme usually runs vertically. When transcendence is projected ahead of us, the scheme takes on a horizontal form. Through vertical projection, permanence is secured, as through horizontal projection, time and change become necessary instruments for the realization of normative value. Thus, there is a tendency in the vertical scheme to understand that the ideals "exist" in their realized state only at the top of the hierarchical ladder, while, in the horizontal scheme, the realized state is projected forward in time.

Looking back on the classical Greek philosophical age, one can observe that the clash between permanence and change formed the subject, as Plato constructs it, of the clash between philosophers represented by the positions of Parmenides and Heraclitus. Parmenides is the philosopher of permanence; Heraclitus the philosopher of time and change. In declaring that "Being is, not-being cannot be," Parmenides was ascribing time and change to the world of illusions. For Parmenides, time and change are unreal, their appearances notwithstanding. For Heraclitus, reality could be likened to a river, or a stream, into which one cannot step twice in the same place.[5] The stream is always moving, never the same from one moment to the next. It is dynamic,

5. Philip Wheelwright translates Heraclitus's fragment 21 as follows: "You cannot step twice into the same river, for other waters are continually flowing on," in his book *Heraclitus* (New York: Atheneum Publishers, 1964), p. 29. Fragment 21 is complemented by fragment 110, "Into the same rivers we step and we do not step" (p. 90).

ever-restive. One cannot position himself by a tree by the side of the stream and expect the situation of the stream to repeat itself even once. The stream is never the same, and neither, according to Heraclitus, is reality. Thus, whereas Parmenides gave normative status to permanence, Heraclitus gave normative status to change. Heraclitus also said that time is like a child playing checkers or draughts.[6] Time makes choices. In stream language, reality is dynamic; its character and shape are formed by moment-to-moment decisions. But the criteria by which decisions are made are not given in advance. The child, unlike the adult, makes up the rules of the game as he goes along. He doesn't know the rules, and therefore must experiment with them, then change them, not quite knowing what it takes to win, who the contestants are, or what the rules are. Something of this is implicit in Heraclitus's imagery—an imagery which is called to mind in Ernst Bloch's declaration that time has invaded the cathedral. And, there is also something of Henri Bergson in Ernst Bloch—Bergson, the chronicler of "creative evolution," who recognized that the fact of time implies that dynamic forces are posed against static ones.

In other language, process has approached the cathedral. It musters the courage to knock on the cathedral's huge, thick doors. Then, it slips inside, at first almost unrecognized. In time, the cathedral will come to feel time's presence. For time has indeed invaded the cathedral. The hope thinkers are very sure of this. They see instances of the occurrence everywhere. And once the invasion has occurred, the cathedral can never be the same. After the invasion, the basis of the cathedral has been shifted onto different ground.

6. In Wheelwright's translation, this affirmation is rendered as follows: "Time is a child moving counters in a game; the royal power is a child's" (fragment 24, p. 29).

The phenomenon repeats itself whenever the proposals of a process thinker are directed toward the identifying characteristics of an established institution. It finds parallels, for example, in the reception originally given to Teilhard de Chardin's proposals by official churchdom, both Catholic and Protestant. Indeed Teilhard's case can itself serve as a kind of chronicle of how "process" fares vis-à-vis permanence-based institutions. Following the initial resistance, following the first awareness that there had been an unanticipated invasion that the cathedral could tolerate only by undergoing its own process of *aggiornamento,* the institution found itself being reformed by the requirements of the process disposition. Gradually, it found those proposals to be both attractive and enervating. Then, in careful sequence, the institution also came to realize that the enervation could not dissolve the fear that the very existence of the institution would be threatened by any concerted attempt on its part to incorporate, contain, or even control the process dynamic. The birth of horizontal innovation throws previously stable things into an eventual disarray.

But it is important that the cathedral imagery be accurately placed. Bloch is not simply talking about inactive cathedrals, located in remote places, centers of refuge for tourists, picture-takers, and historians of antiquated institutions. It is not the cathedral become museum, nor the cathedral at a distance, but a cathedral which affects and qualifies human lives. Humanity lives in and by the cathedral. The cathedral is full of people, and particularly at times of festival. Indeed, not only does the cathedral "summarize" culture; it also "contains" people. And this, as the hope thinkers see it, is its great liability. As they look at it, recalling Plato's imagery of the cave, the people which the cathedral contains are contained by the cathedral.

Because reality cannot be so contained—not, that is, if time is real—such people must be freed to join forces with the fuller reality which pertains outside the cathedral. Unlike the cave, however, the cathedral is not lost in shadows, appearances, images, and mere glimpses of reality (although the mirror should not be confused with that which it mirrors). The cathedral is not deficient in the sense that in screening off reality it prevents its inhabitants from seeing what is really there. Bloch, unlike Plato, cannot tell his story of contrasts in terms of the opposition between darkness and light, as though the cathedral, like the cave, harbors darkness while the true light comes from beyond its borders. Rather, the chief weakness of the cathedral is that it is not mobile and labile. It is a cathedral when it ought to be a ship. If it were a ship, it would be fitted for passage. And, if fitted for passage, it would know how to move properly. The task, then, is to provide the cathedral with seaworthiness. This is necessary if the cathedral is to survive in a world of process, in which reality's substratum, if one can call it that, is ever-restive and undergoing a perpetual process of innovation. The cathedral must become like a ship because in place of permanence there are simply more or less reliable places of relative security this side of arrival at harbor. Cathedrals can be fitted to landscapes, but water is associated with the origin and flow of life. Thus, in shifting from cathedrals to ships, the hope movement tends to replace terrestrial with aquatic imagery. And the cathedral, which had already transformed the cave, has been turned into a vessel built for a long but deliberate voyage. The divine comedy is being staged in odyssean terms.

According to the analogy, then, cathedrals are landmarks —beautifully impressive landmarks—from a time when it was deemed important to fix a place on the land. But, seen from voyage perspectives, they are deceptive, for settling a place should not be construed as being equivalent to catching permanence. Permanence can neither be captured nor contained even in durable edifices. For Bloch, Moltmann, and Metz, there is a certain psychological, emotional, and religious release in just knowing that. They are not giddy, but neither are they somber.[7] Thus, Bloch notices that when time invades the cathedral, the cathedral is not simply torn down. Time does not destroy the cathedral. Rather, the cathedral's vertical extensions remain, but in revised dimensionality. Extension is put on its side, as it were, and projected horizontally rather than vertically. This must be, Bloch notes, because the goal for humanity, even for those within the cathedral, lies at some distance away. The goal is reserved for the future. Distance has to be traversed if the ship is to arrive at the harbor. And the harbor is not wherever the ship happens to be, nor is the ship the harbor. The harbor is still at some distance from the location of the ship. The goal is not simply to be lodged securely within either ship or cathedral, but to arrive resolutely and safely at the harbor. And the space between the present situation of the ship and the harbor is largely uncharted, that is, until the ship traverses it. The ship gives space form, but the ship itself is not that form.

It is almost as if the imagery were that employed by John Henry Cardinal Newman's hymn "Lead Kindly Light" which was originally written as Newman contemplated a homeward journey from faraway Sicily: "I do not ask to see the distant scene; one step enough for me." Or, perhaps the best analogue is neither Plato's cave nor Newman's prayer,

7. Cf. Jürgen Moltmann's lecture "How Can I Play When I'm in a Strange Land?" trans. M. Douglas Meeks, in *Kalamazoo College Review* 32, no. 3 (1970): 17–24.

but the figure of Noah. It was Noah who, when the earth was filled with violence, found favor in God's eyes, and was party to a covenant which focused on the fitting of an ark, an instrument of passage. But when one thinks of Noah, one also thinks of Abraham, the proto-pilgrim father of Israel, the nomad, the wanderer. But with Abraham, there is also Moses, the leader of the exodus, who, at the same time, was debarred from entering the land of Canaan, the one chosen to bring the oppressed people out of bondage into freedom. Certainly Bloch has combined images of pilgrims from Jewish history with conceptualizations of process from early Greek philosophy. In giving title to those images, he might be saying that both history and reality take form in the passage from possibility to actuality, from diffusion to identity. But some who hear him also detect that Bloch is not simply describing historical personages, nor sketching in the context out of which oppressions are overcome. He is even doing more than talking about personal self-consciousness, and some processes by which ego-integrity is effected. In very truth, Bloch is also giving form to a disposition which, some say, can even be applied to God himself. God, in being "I will be who I will be," can also be depicted according to the process economy. Hence, the cathedral within which men worship the God "who will be" must of necessity become a vessel fitted for passage. To be formed in any other way is to stand in opposition to its fundamental raison d'être.

TWO

Ernst Bloch:
Steward of Hopes,
Dreams, Mysteries

Space and time, color and form, are but ways of seeing that
stem from the transient structure of our own souls. Space is
a conceived projection of our own beings. Time is an esti-
mate of our being, into which we introduce the concept of
"the present" as an imaginary quantity.   —Franz Marc

The new is never totally new. It is always preceded by a
dream, a promise, an anticipation. He who does not expect
the unexpected does not find it.   —Ernst Bloch

Without Ernst Bloch there would probably be no hope
school. Or, if there were one, without Bloch, it would probably not be known. Without doubt, Bloch's writings (chiefly
his three-volume book *Das Prinzip Hoffnung*) are the
school's primary stimulus. And yet there is irony in this, for
the school which Bloch prompted has not been established
to give systematic articulation to his thought; indeed, his
thought does not yield to systematic representation. Furthermore, most of those thinkers who work under the
banner of whatever school of hope there is have not worked
directly under Bloch, nor, in many cases, are they conversant in all of the subjects he has treated. But more
curious than this is the probability that Ernst Bloch himself

would never join a school of hope, even the one which his thoughts have prompted, or even one which was organized under his hand. He does not quite belong there, for the lines along which schools develop are different from the lines along which many of Ernst Bloch's interests run. It is not really the case that he is larger than any school he might inspire, but, more accurately, that he cannot be contained. Just as his thought cannot be systematized, so also does his disposition elude any sort of formal ordering.[1] He simply cannot be set to program, but the sparks which he ignites travel in many directions and can be used to enlighten a host of possibilities and to search out new ones of which most men had no awareness before.

A great part of hope's current appeal derives from the intrigue which surrounds Bloch, the Jewish, atheistic, Marxist revisionist, several-times refugee, former part-time dishwasher, utopian theoretician whose book *Das Prinzip Hoffnung*[2] is the movement's recent stimulus. Bloch has color, as well as a mysteriousness and courageousness which attracts attention and insures that anything to which he gives his name will be pervaded by an element of surprise. He is

1. With reference to Bloch's tendency to resist any systematization of thought, Jürgen Moltmann writes, "Old stories, recondite fairy-tales, and philosophical profundities mingle with journalistic topicality, criticism of the times, and political purpose. It is a transitional form of thought, expressed with a vocabulary and style that are always provocative and startling. Here no theoretical system is built up like an old Gothic cathedral, stone by stone, as if to afford an encyclopedia of the whole. Bloch wants his thinking to be 'transcending'; and to bring the new and unknown of the future into the proximity of the lived moment. This thinking serves the ends of practice, experience, and change. It moves like a ship that never stays in one place and yet holds an unvarying direction. It is full of the mysticism of the obscure, lived moment; and yet the thinker's eyes are open to fleeting encounters and superficial peculiarities. 'To have plumbed thought at its deepest is to love life at its quickest,' said Hölderlin" (Jürgen Moltmann, "Introduction," in Ernst Bloch, *Man On His Own*, trans. E. B. Ashton [New York: Herder and Herder, 1970], pp. 21–22).

2. Ernst Bloch, *Das Prinzip Hoffnung*, 3 vols. (Frankfurt: Suhrkamp Verlag, 1959).

both an avant-garde thinker and a thinker of avant-gardisms. And the power of his suggestions seems to express itself in the proliferation of still other suggestions on the part of those who read or hear him. He is a creative thinker who possesses the ability to say new things in new ways, old things in new ways, and new things in old ways. To call him a creative thinker, however, is not necessarily to call him a careful or meticulous thinker. The power in his thought lies in the vitality of his suggestions, but one runs aground when he tries to commit such thought to a consistent pattern or system.

Like Immanuel Kant before him, Ernst Bloch knows that the question about hope, "for what may I hope," arises within the context of aesthetics. From the outset, this supplies his writing with stories, myths, and folklore. He knows this as a philosopher; and, as a writer, he knows how to make that correlation operational. His books are filled with images, allegories, stories, and folklore.[3] In addition, he is unwilling to turn such things into anything else. Indeed, his proposals are couched in aesthetic terminology. He is a storyteller and a painter of verbal images. His thought is expressed through the succession of images which he places before the reader. He seems to be aware, as others have contended, that the artist is the first person in a culture to glimpse the configuration of the future. And he employs this awareness in the accounts which he renders. One would almost suspect that Bloch thinks in pictures. It is as though the world itself is pictorial. It is also optical. Bloch knows about projection, and about the perceptual

---

3. Moltmann says, "Bloch is a master of the art of narrative which makes the familiar sound baffling, and brings out unexpected and quite different aspects of the conventional. He thinks in narration, and surprises in colloquy; he baffles, attracts, provokes, mystifies, and unveils at the same time" ("Introduction," p. 23).

structure of illusion. His world is composed of the dreams men commit to daylight. The trouble with most men, he believes, is that they don't take the world of images, dreams, and pictorial displays seriously enough. Even those who take dreams seriously are wont to converting dreams into something else. They make dreams the basis of analyzing inner mental states, or treat them as reliable means of access to previous childhood frustration. Some men have learned to take night dreams seriously, but daydreaming, Bloch feels, is hardly ever recognized as a source of personal or corporate insight. However, Bloch believes that it is from the world of images that the future takes form. Hence dreams and images are able to delineate heretofore unrealized possibilities. For him, there is no future except the future which is dreamed for. If such a future is going to be, men must be able to dream it first, or anticipate it, at least in fantasy or illusion. The next step involves giving substance to fantasy and content to illusion.[4] Bloch hopes that men will come to mediate the future that way. He prides himself on being able to view the world as though it were being pulled ahead by the future.

Consequently, Bloch also views the present world metaphorically. Human history is a journey, and man is at once a pilgrim and a voyager. The world in process is a world understood as a venture. The pilgrim's part in that venture is to effect light for the world. The light expands in both intensity and scope as one approximates the end. As the voyager sees it, the end is also home.

Standing back, the analyst can observe that these are characteristic tendencies of patterns of thought which use the materials of a horizontal conceptual model. In every

4. Appropriately, then, Ivo Frenzel entitles his discussion of Bloch's thought, "Philosophie zwischen Traum und Apokalypse," in *Über Ernst Bloch* (Frankfurt: Suhrkamp Verlag, 1968), pp. 17–41.

instance, without exception, man is depicted in terms of linear progression. Thus man receives his role by reference to a normative process which moves toward a desired *telos*. With respect to the process, man is participant; and with respect to the end point, he is agent. Thus, a man's career is formed by the same set of forces over which he must exercise control, and which he must guide toward the realization of higher purposes. The individual is defined by the very process which he must also shape, in order to maximize development and progress. Thus, man understands himself to have been placed on a continuum, a continuum marked by the integers of time. Because of the continuum, the future emerges as something entirely credible, and as something to which man has access. The continuum's capacity to remain flexible—at least flexible enough to admit a future which, in a chronological sense, is "still not yet"— gives realism to man's hope.

Three formal ingredients are necessary to the conceptualization of linear progression.[5] First, the *process* itself is necessary. Without the process, the scheme would lose its basic structural component; it is this component which gives extensibility to reflection, and determines that the scale to which reflection will be arranged will run horizontally rather than vertically. Second, the scheme needs *possibility*.[6] As process is necessary to give direction and force, so

5. For an analysis of the conceptual structure of Bloch's thought, see Egenolf Roeder von Diersburg, *Zur Ontologie und Logik offener Systeme: Ernst Bloch vor dem Gesetz der Tradition* (Hamburg: Felix Meiner Verlag, 1967). For an analysis of the structure of "the process model" more generally, see Newton P. Stallknecht and Robert S. Brumbaugh, *The Compass of Philosophy: An Essay in Intellectual Orientation* (New York: Longmans, Green and Company, 1954), chapter five, "Creative Becoming," pp. 133–76.

6. The centrality of "possibility" (*möglichkeit*) to Bloch's thought is underscored in Hellmuth G. Bütow's study, *Philosophie und Gesellschaft im Denken Ernst Blochs* (Berlin: Otto Harrassowitz, 1963), pp. 133–42.

possibility is necessary to give character and style to the process. Possibility functions, first, as a means by which the process gains forward aspiration, and, second, as a primary source of the content which gets inscribed within the process. The process acts as context and receptor of the possibilities which, sooner or later, are written into it. Third, the scheme needs an agent to facilitate the transition from possibility as possibility to a possibility which is realized and concretized in the process itself. The agent is always a decision maker, for it is called upon to select from existing possibilities those possibilities which are to be fitted to the ongoing process. The agent is also in some sense creator. By means of his ability to effect a meeting between possibility and process the effective agent becomes a molder of the process, or, a practitioner of the process. And in the reality of possibility, there is a place for man's dreams and hopes. Both dreams and hopes can be negotiated because of the open future whose delineation rests upon human decision. In more precise terms, hope and dreams must be taken seriously because they serve as sources of insight to which reference is made when decisions are reached, which decisions imply that possibilities have taken up residence in the future-tending process.

In some versions of conceptual models which run horizontally, a fourth formal ingredient is defined, namely, the end or final destination toward which the process moves. In every instance, the final end is implicit; in some, however, it is also specified. Consequently, some process thinkers argue that the final end is simply the perpetuation of possibility, so that the enrichment procedures never ever run out. Others see a more definite end, the achievement of specific goals. But, for all, the end is freedom—freedom as freedom, or freedom as the final and unassailable positioning of a definitive "we community."[7] In other words, the end point is always infused with openness. It may be a state of unlimited openness—that is, openness without qualification.[8] Or, on the other hand, it may be the ascription of free and unlimited reign to a particular group of people. Bloch himself chooses to depict the end in the following terms: "The meaning of human history already there from the start is the building of the commonwealth of freedom."[9] The choice of words "commonwealth of freedom" combines the two senses of freedom and openness referred to above. There is specification, in that the end has reference to a definite entity, namely, a people whose communal form and eventual occurrence are understood to be ideal. And there is also freedom, in that the community has been given a perpetual openness which is qualified by no previous restraints.

In spite of his combination maverick and inventive bent, Ernst Bloch can be regarded as a thinker whose program follows a typical pattern. His views are formed by a perspective which includes the three necessary formal ingredients. In the first place, the world has a fundamental underlying élan. As he puts it repeatedly, the world is on a "process course." Secondly, the world process is formed by possibility. The process is referred to as venture because the course is not prefixed, but, instead, is a product of the kind of experimentation which makes openness perpetual.

7. I have treated the concept of "we community" at greater length, though without particular reference to Ernst Bloch, in "Segerstedt on We-Feeling: A Refinement of Comfort-Challenge," forthcoming in *Acta Sociologica*. The most thorough analysis of Bloch's idea of "community" of which I am aware is Bütow's study, *Philosophie und Gesellschaft im Denken Ernst Blochs*.

8. The category "openness" (*offenheit*) is given thorough discussion in Egenolf Roeder von Diersburg, *Zur Ontologie und Logik offener Systeme*, especially pp. 1–8.

9. Ernst Bloch, *A Philosophy of the Future*, trans. John Cumming (New York: Herder and Herder, 1970), p. 138.

Thirdly, Bloch has a place for the agents who effect the actualization of possibility within the process. Such agents are men (identified sometimes as corporate human awareness) who bring light to the world's stream and underscore all of it with refreshment. And, finally, as we have already observed, Bloch says much about the end toward which the process is tending. It has a final destination, one which is implicit in its fiber. Seen as a whole, the world's stream can be understood as a tendential event. Because of the presence of all of these formal factors, Bloch's outlook looks very much like the philosophical positions of Henri Bergson, Alfred North Whitehead, and, with much refinement, both Georg W. F. Hegel and Teilhard de Chardin.[10] All of these view the world in dynamic terms; for them the world is in process of movement, and the movement occurs on a continuum whose integers can be marked and whose direction always has destination.

But, in addition to being a somewhat typical thinker, Ernst Bloch is also a very special one. Every thinker of process analogies must eventually name the principal stuff by which the process is comprised, and he must also provide an account of the motivation which is responsible for its forward-tending. That basic stuff may be physical or ontological, or it might be historical and/or mental. It may be that reality itself, to use the common jargon, is in process. Or, it may be that the continuum of human history is dynamically involved in the realization of deep-seated objectives. Similarly, one may decide that human beings are progressing toward a state of increased self-consciousness. Or, he may conceive of the motivation as an innate natural drive, perhaps as "survival of the species," or even a tendency toward maximizing such aesthetic factors as

10. I have explored the structural similarities between Bloch's and a host of others' thought in "Vertical v. Horizontal Theology: Bloch-Dewart-Irenaeus," in *Continuum* 5, no. 4 (1968): 616–33.

purpose, harmony, and order, or as the removal of all impediments to freedom.

When it comes to decisions of this kind, Ernst Bloch reveals another side of his eclectic bent. To a high degree, he discloses his acceptance of the basic Hegelian outlook. From one side, the stuff of his process is historical; that is, he trains his eye on the movement of history, particularly the history of the Western world, from the classical Greek period to the present day. From his vantage point, Western history itself is a continuum which tends toward a hoped-for (though not dialectically inevitable) culmination. But, from another side, that same historical process mirrors a dialectic of development, a maturation of self-consciousness, which recalls Hegel's *Phenomenology of the Spirit.* And the drama being played out within self-consciousness, in turn, reflects the dynamic interplay written into intellectual culture. Consequently, at one and the same time, Bloch is involved in writing socio-historical criticism, reflections on human awareness, and descriptions of the processes by which ideological innovations are effected. Because the same pattern pervades all of these, the three accounts are virtually slices of one and the same portrayal. The three accounts become three ways of focusing on alienation. And, in all three instances the dialectic is formed by the rhythms of conflict and mediation.

Of course, Bloch's attitudes to human history have been influenced by the writings of Karl Marx.[11] As is well known,

11. Bloch's relationship to Marxism, and his dependence on the thought of Karl Marx, is explored at length in the following studies: Jürgen Rühle, "The Philosopher of Hope: Ernst Bloch," in *Revisionism: Essays on the History of Marxist Ideas,* ed. Leopold Labedz (New York: Frederick A. Praeger, 1962), pp. 166–78; and Hellmuth G. Bütow, *Philosophie und Gesellschaft im Denken Ernst Blochs.* Ivo Frenzel argues that Bloch stands to Marx as Socrates stands to the Sophists, Aristotle to Plato, Thomas Aquinas to Averroes, Kant to the empiricists, and Heidegger to Neo-Kantianism and phenomenology, in "Philosophie zwischen Traum und Apokalypse," pp. 19–20.

Marx, using economic factors as the prime criterion, understands alienation to refer to the estrangement of the worker
in an industrial and capitalistic society. That estrangement
is regarded as a pervasive human fact, and is mirrored in
the political, moral, and religious domains as well. When its
prime religious implications are drawn, they are done so by
means of Ludwig Feuerbach's contention that the arrange-
ments between man and God must be altered. As Feuerbach
saw it, the vertical hierarchization of the God-world relationship must become inverted if man is to be given a
proper place. Under Marxist interpretation, ownership of
property becomes the crucial issue. It is the obligation
of property owners to protect their interests even by legal
safeguards. Consequently, if those who do not own property
are to redress their grievances against their superiors, they
have no recourse except revolutionary action. Those who
are subservient must become emancipated; but emancipa-
tion is possible only through an overhauling of the conditions of the feudal economy. The responsibility for pro-
duction must be taken away from the propertied class and
put under the agency of the workers.

The same kind of reversal must occur in the distinctively
religious domain. The God who preserves the position of
the propertied, who safeguards the status quo while holding
out transcendent (but nonconcrete) comforts to the poor,
must be replaced by concerted human effort to better man's
fundamental condition. Thus, instead of expending energy
or lending devotion and subordinating oneself to some
transcendent deity, who is nothing more than the religious
device of the propertied classes, men should effectively
orient themselves toward other men and devote themselves
toward creating a workable "heaven on earth." Moreover,
instead of projecting human need upward—toward God,

beyond man—men should recognize human need for what it is, then work to alleviate it. Ultimately, the projection of human need skyward is simply a disguised form of lack of courage; it is nothing more than a selling-out to fictitious higher powers. One can explain this entire religious tendency by reference to the tacit acknowledgment that one has been placed under the rule of that which lies outside his power of control. Under such a regime, religion functions to give sanction to the exploitation of those who do not own property and are not economically privileged. Religion, in effect, is an instrument to keep poor people poor, and, by the same token, to maintain the status of the wealthy.

Bloch agrees with the Marxist-Feuerbachian view that the pervasive social inequities must be redressed by the kind of revolutionary action which leads to a deposing of the hierarchical scheme. According to Feuerbach and Marx, the bipolar relationship must be reversed. That which was placed at the top of the hierarchy formerly must be seen for what it really is, namely, human possibility, and must be brought back down, historically actualized and economically concretized. The feudal system—both socio-politically and theologically—must be destroyed, and the community of men working with men must replace the impotent sighs of frustration and disappointment which result when the responsibility for bringing about that mythological, transcendent, far-off, faraway, heavenly, permanent, eternal kingdom is left solely to the almighty work of God. In reversing the hierarchical order, Bloch also attempts to sacralize man by ridding human value of any theistic dependence. His goal, in short, is to depose the God of permanence.

But Bloch also quarrels with Marx. In general tendency, the thought of the two political theorists follows the same lines. In specific terms, however, Bloch criticizes Marx for not being revolutionary enough, almost in the same way that Marx had earlier criticized his predecessors for theorizing about the world rather than discovering ways of changing it. Marx's mistake, as Bloch sees it, is to make economics into a reductionistic norm. In Marx's view, economics is determinative of everything else. Disagreeing with that contention, Bloch writes as follows:

> By itself, of course, the sobriety of such a view is ultimately barren. Man does not live by bread alone. Outward things, no matter how extensive their importance and our need to attend to them, are merely suggestive, not creative. People, not things and not the mighty course of events outside ourselves (which Marx falsely places above us), write history.[12]

By turning attention away from things toward people, Bloch is not denying the fact that alienation is the fundamental human dilemma. But he is suggesting that the dilemma cannot simply be reduced to the economic factor implicit in the inevitable conflict between classes of people. The reality of the conflict there testifies to an equally pervasive and deep-seated split within man's subjective self. What Bloch denies is that economic determinism is sufficient to give form and tone to both culture and moral life. In other words, for Bloch it is not enough to redesign the reciprocity between producer and consumer; reconstruction in that domain is a never-ending task. Beyond that, it is also necessary to supply the personal human quotient with the functional equivalents of the God the Marxist inversion banished. Men should assume responsibility for filling in the ranks of possibility left vacant when the gods were deposed. As Bloch sees it, the Marxist dialectic "has voided

12. Ernst Bloch, "Karl Marx, Death and the Apocalypse," in *Man On His Own,* p. 37.

the economy, but the soul and faith it was to make room for are missing."[13]

In the end, then, economic reductionisms make for a barren world, a world "without the music we ought to hear." Mystery has been lost, or at least replaced, by "an ideology for very sober class purposes and economic upheavals." And the "Marxist fixations or an atheistic *status quo* that offers the human soul nothing more than a more or less eudaimonistically furnished 'heaven on earth'," has led to an inability to recognize persistent, necessary, and fundamental religious aspirations.

> Throughout all the movements and goals of worldly transformation, there has been a desire to make room for life, for the attainment of a divine essence, for men to integrate themselves at last, in a millennium, with human kindness, freedom, and the light of the *telos*.[14]

The Marxist revolution, as Bloch sees it, has not properly aligned itself with the utopian élan. As a consequence, it has become impoverished because of the selective attention it gives to economic conditions. It has not drawn on the magnificent resourcefulness of the full-bodied utopian disposition. In dispelling "heaven" in the hierarchical sense it also loses touch with "heaven" in the utopian sense. Bloch brands it "half-enlightenment," not full enlightenment, for it has effectively exercised criticism but without gaining an inheritance. It was successful in stimulating upheaval, but without being properly able to submit constructive and creative plans regarding that to which the upheaval was meant to give ground. Thus Bloch can say that "Marxism is near to being a critique of pure reason for which no critique

13. Ibid., p. 39.
14. Ibid.

of practical reason has yet been written."[15] In Kantian terms, something was denied in order to make room for something else. But Marx offered a denial which has not yet made room for anything.

Bloch's correction of Marx's thought implies moving to a new subject. It is not enough to talk about the dynamics of economic interchange, for the larger context is the many-faceted, multi-layered world of human subjectivity. The range of economics properly determined and the inclination of the human heart, as noted earlier, can be regarded as slices of the same phenomenon. Bloch approaches both with a view toward overcoming alienation. And, where self-consciousness is concerned, such alienation has reference to the contrast between inner and outer experience. Thus, the two strands—Bloch's analysis of human history and his treatment of subjectivity—are kept together through the thesis that utopia is finally universal self-encounter. The analysis runs as follows:

The goal of the subjective life of man, as Bloch sees it, is the realization of the self. The self which is meant to be is potentially there at all times; hence, its becoming occurs as the inner is made outer, or as inclinations are exteriorized. But the relation between inner and outer cannot be understood in simplistic fashion, as though inner is always chronologically prior and outer is always product or expression. The movement from inner to outer is complicated by the fact that its controlling tendency is toward the *novum*. Hence, while it is proper to speak of the potential-self becoming actual-self it is also appropriate to speak of that sequence of events in terms of the "genesis of the beginning."[16] The inner becomes outer as the beginning becomes.

15. Ibid.
16. Ernst Bloch, "Incipit Vita Nova," in *Man On His Own*, p. 92.

The logic of the transformation of self-consciousness is complex, but the thrust is easily discernible when viewed in the light of the *telos*. The final goal is "the building of the commonwealth of freedom."[17] That goal is corporate, rather than simply individual, and, at the same time, it implies the reconciliation of subject and object. What is internal in man—his hopes, his aspirations, all of which presumes his primary utopian urge, for man is a hoping animal—will eventually assume external form. It becomes the substance of the anticipated "commonwealth." Hence, seen from the point of view of the *telos*, the distinction between inner and outer is modal only, and not substantive. As self-consciousness grows, so also is the "commonwealth of freedom" articulated. But the process by which both are effected is not simply that of dialectical inevitability. On the contrary, the language Bloch uses at this point in his discussion is distinctively religious rather than methodological. He speaks, for example, of rebirth, of the "dynamic" (and not only allegorical) process of dying and "transformation," and his intention is clarified in the following passage:

> A clear distinction must be made between renewal and the new life. For renewal implies recourse to what has been (however inimical it may be to what has since come to be); whereas the new life implies advance toward what has as yet never appeared. . . .[18]

The transforming process, then, is not merely resuscitation, or a winning back of something previously possessed but

17. In elucidating his notion of "the commonwealth of freedom" Bloch speaks expressly about "the 'we-problem' of collectivity as such" in "Karl Marx, Death and the Apocalypse," p. 42, which, in the original, was referred to as "Wirproblem" ("Karl Marx, der Tod und die Apokalypse," in *Geist der Utopie* [Frankfurt: Suhrkamp Verlag, 1964], p. 308).

18. Bloch, "Incipit Vita Nova," p. 80.

subsequently lost. Rather, it consists of a progressive involvement in the *novum*. It is the way of coming to terms with the beginning. It is, as it were, a turning toward the beginning. Or, in other words, it is an exercising of renovation, yes, even revolution, within the subjective life of man.

Through his description of all of it, Bloch holds true to the thesis that the inner gives access to the outer:

That which is within is and remains the key to that which is without; yet the key is not the substance, but the substance of the key as well is in the object-house (as yet hardly on its way to completion) that is the world.[19]

The key, of course, pinpoints the sources of inner insight, not only mediation, but fantasy, dreams, even visions and projections, as well as discursive, hard-nosed reflection. In such phenomena one finds the stirrings which eventuate in commonwealths of freedom. But those anticipations are also present in youth ("genuine youth has everything in front of itself, and seizes that fact. It has forfeited itself to the new . . ."),[20] as well as in productivity and creativity. Bloch also sees that which is not yet conscious appearing in "time shifts," or in the transitions between eras, epochs, and ages. In all such cases, something is brought to the threshold of the "still not yet," then carried forward in openness toward external concretization. And as the unconscious (or preconscious) is made conscious, so also is the universal religious utopian tendency made visible.

Bloch is a political theorist, to be sure, but he is also a craftsman of artistic thought. The best clue one has to the sense of his contentions, therefore, is probably not the writings of Karl Marx or Ludwig Feuerbach as much as the

19. Bloch, *A Philosophy of the Future,* p. 36.
20. Ernst Bloch, "Man as Possibility," in *The Future of Hope,* ed. Walter H. Capps (Philadelphia: Fortress Press, 1970), p. 64.

principles of expressionist art by which his early thought was decidedly influenced, which influence he has always honored.[21] In saying that the inner gives access to the outer, and not the reverse, Bloch is repeating a dominant expressionist contention, namely, that space and time are formed primarily by personal, emotive factors. As expressionists see it, the world is a composition; it is a visualization of inner sensations, inclinations, emotions, and thoughts. The task of the artist—taken here as the paradigm for both creative and cultural work—is to project the content of the imagination onto a visual plane, and, thereby, to liberate inward vision and aesthetic sensitivity from previously established patterns of articulation. The artist works, then, not simply to create art for art's sake, but, more profoundly, to be an agent in effecting social change. The goal is social revolution. Thus, the communication of immediate feelings is to serve social change, and the rhythms which compose man's inner, personal history are to be turned outward to transform man's social and cultural history. The outer world's

21. Bloch's views on art and aesthetics are a subject in their own right. Throughout his writings, Bloch makes reference to such expressionist artists as Franz Marc, Paul Klee, and Wassily Kandinsky. He also shares the expressionist ideology, i.e., that there is an otherworldly, not-material reality, accessible to intuitional seeking, which lies beyond the mechanized world. Many of Bloch's views regarding art are included in his essay "Philosophie der Kunst," in his *Subjekt-Objekt* (Frankfurt: Suhrkamp Verlag, 1962), pp. 274–313, although in this essay Bloch works from a Hegelian basis rather than from expressionist tendencies. For descriptions and interpretations of expressionism, see Charles L. Kuhn, *German Expressionism and Abstract Art* (Cambridge: Harvard University Press, 1957), especially Kuhn's essay, "Survey of Modern German Art," pp. 3–17, and Jakob Rosenberg's essay, "German Graphic Art of the Twentieth Century," pp. 21–30; Bernard S. Myers, *The German Expressionists. A Generation in Revolt* (New York: Frederick A. Praeger, 1957); and the article "Expressionism" in *Encyclopedia of World Art*, vol. 5 (New York: McGraw-Hill, 1961), pp. 311–23. Bloch's relationship to expressionism is made visible, through the lines, in John Willett's book, *Expressionism* (London: Weidenfeld and Nicolson, 1970), which includes a comprehensive bibliography which gives special attention to English-language books on the subject, pp. 248–52.

configuration is to emanate from a conscious extension of the style of man's inward awareness. The world, in short, must be changed; and the changes are to come by design.

Of course, the source of the world's design is the perpetually creative human imagination. Little by little, men learn the imaginative techniques of converting psychological drives into potent and formative poetic forces. Thus, through the conversion, the visual, pictorial world is a derivative of emotional self-awareness. Life produces form, and the language of forms issues from the mystery of living. August Macke, one of the expressionist theoreticians, put it, "to create form is to live."[22] The outer world results from the translation of imaginative insights into perceptual structures. Thus, the interpretation of the world always resides in its imaginative design. Indeed, the design of the world is its interpretation. The world takes on configuration when deep-seated inner tendencies are brought together, then visually displayed on an external plane. Ultimately, then, the salvation of the world, as the expressionist sees it, refers to the orchestrative capacities of the artist. Social reformation requires the cultivation of artistic talents. The artist can serve as social reformer because the "stuff" of the world is of aesthetic origin.

The language Bloch chooses for much of his description is visual and optical, and seizes upon water imagery. In referring to Nietzsche's summons "Embark!" for example, he describes the voyage which that summons implies as carrying one "through the outside world . . . to new waters."[23] In other passages, he refers frequently to "currents" and "streams," indeed even to "the current of the

22. August Macke, statement cited in "Expressionism" in *Encyclopedia of World Art,* p. 319.
23. Bloch, *A Philosophy of the Future,* p. 37.

world's stream."[24] Similarly, the voyage to which he refers repeatedly is one which transverses an ocean; he says, for example, that "a voyage in the training ship (is) more effective than the onshore lecture."[25] And perhaps nowhere is water imagery more prevalent than in the following passage:

> The world is developing in history, and continuously coming forth; yet as it does so, it leaves its history behind. The sun of Homer (or of Hegel, or of Marx) will shine (no physical sun) only if at each dawn in history it rises anew from the spreading ocean.[26]

And even when the analogues are not expressly aquatic, the terminology is always that of the voyage. Man is a pilgrim, a voyager, a participant in a journey. As the ship sails for a distant harbor, a harbor which its navigational instruments can plot on the horizon even though it is not yet visible, so also is man tending toward home. As Bloch puts it, "*Homo semper tiro*: man is always a beginner; the world is a venture; and man's part is to give it light."[27] Tending toward the place of self-identity, man participates in the process which links exodus and homecoming, New Year's Eve and New Year's Day. Of course, the journey itself is the mediation of the *novum*, which, in turn, is the presentation of the beginning. But, at the same time, the journey or voyage effects the reconciliation of inner and outer, subject and object. Man does not yet know who he is until he reaches the place of self-identity. Thus, in his introductory biography of Bloch, Jürgen Moltmann cites that thesis as support for the contention that *biographical* remarks must be made with great caution: "Man is still

24. Ibid., p. 48.
25. Ibid., p. viii.
26. Bloch, "Incipit Vita Nova," p. 84.
27. Bloch, *A Philosophy of the Future,* p. viii.

undetermined being; hence a certain reserve is advisable in biographical notes. Ernst Bloch was born in Ludwigshafen in 1885. . . ."[28] That is all. But the voyage itself is the exercise in which self-awareness comes to maturity.

When the metaphorical language is studied, Bloch's contention seems to add up to the following description of human experience. Man is a wayfarer, and the world is a process. The voyage is necessary if several fundamental forms of alienation are to be mediated rather than overcome. One dominant form of alienation is economic, and has reference to class exploitation. It derives primarily from the several kinds of interdependency which are implicit in ownership of property. Those who do not own property are economically dependent on those who do. And those who do own property are responsible for perpetuating their estate and maintaining support of their vested interests. A related form of alienation has to do with the conflict between subject and object—between internal aspiration and resolve, and external circumstances. Once again there is disparity as well as antagonism between decisions or conscious choices, on the one hand, and the seemingly fixed outer fabric in which the products of conscientious behavior come to register. In principle, Bloch believes that both forms of alienation can only be overcome through a kind of exchange; in the first place, the possessions of "the haves" must be taken away and made the property of "the have nots"; and, in the second place, the primary subjective dispositions must take form in the external world. Bloch effects both transformations by employing the distinction between potentiality and actuality, and by taking innovative steps with the categories and tenses of time. Thus, on the one hand, the realm vacated by the gods through Feuerbach's and Marx's inversion has been filled with possibility, that is,

28. Moltmann, "Introduction," p. 21.

possibilities which lean toward specific determination. And, on the other hand, the subject-object dichotomy is mediated when the future is treated as an objective possibility which can also be represented in man's consciousness. But the uniqueness of Bloch's position is implicit in his tendency to refer the beginning to the future rather than to locate it in the past. In tending toward future possibility, man is disposed toward a beginning whose genesis is being enacted in man's tending toward it. Because the "still not yet" is also the beginning, man finds himself a voyager on a venture whose terminus can only be dimly glimpsed. But he knows that when the *telos* is unveiled, the exploitation of man by man will have ceased, and the several forms of alienation and estrangement will have been satisfactorily mediated.

And this introduces the third of the three preselected contexts for Ernst Bloch, in which fundamental alienation must be overcome. Alienation was a fact of natural history, of subjective self-awareness, and, next, also of Western man's corporate history. But this is simply another way of saying that the mediation of estrangement, for Bloch, is never simply an individual matter. The spirit of utopia is also construed in group or collective terms. Man's final destination is not the disclosure of any solitary self, but the building of a human city, Bloch's "commonwealth of freedom."

Two large ramifications follow, or, perhaps it is but one large ramification which can be seen from two sides. First, because the journey is one in which mankind itself is engaged, its underlying process is always recapitulative. The process must serve as the vehicle—indeed, the carrier or vessel—in which corporate mankind is brought forward. Second, because the process is recapitulative, time takes on the dimensions of circularity. The cyclical nature of time results from a juxtaposition of beginning and first points in the series. Because the beginning is projected toward the future, time is called upon to do double duty. On the one hand, it must provide continuity between now and the *novum* so that the two can be connected by a measurable process. In that capacity, time lends reality to the process; it gives credence to the affirmation that the periods of the voyage prior to the future are real. But, simultaneously, time must also preserve the uniqueness of the *novum*. In doing both, time certifies that the *novum*—the point, age, and place toward which the process is tending—gathers up and actualizes every occurrence in the previous sequence which stands to it according to the relation of potentiality and actuality. And it also attributes to those occurrences their own intrinsic position and status which the dawning of the *novum* can neither nullify nor erase.

Of course, the ascription of recapitulative powers to the *novum* is a ploy which is not unique to Bloch's scheme. He is well aware of the recapitulative function of "recollection" in the Platonic tradition, the function of "memory" in Augustinianism, and he notices that "memoirs" characteristically take narrative form (precisely to enjoy recapitulative capacities). The memoir becomes an autobiographical journey back through the stages of self-formation, or a second enactment of the journey itself. Even Hegel's *Phenomenology of the Spirit* can be understood in this way for Bloch, namely, as a biography of human consciousness in general. Bloch's process also functions in a recollective capacity; it gathers up all predecessor events, and eventually brings them to self-awareness in the *novum*. In this respect, as already indicated, Bloch's stance is similar to many others. Indeed, it can be stated as a general rule that the horizontal model of reflection always manifests a "recapitulative" or "recollective" tendency when its termini are coordinated with each other and not simply arbitrarily fixed. "Recapitulation" is always present when a concerted attempt is made to link the end of the process with its beginning.[29] In diagrammatical terms, that is, with reference to thought as modeled, the bringing of end and beginning points together always adds a cyclical dimension to linear succession. The basic process always implies linear progression. Indeed, by means of linear progression, the forward movement of the process is allowed to proceed. But the cyclical dimension is also necessary if the end of the process is to be joined to the beginning. The presence of the cyclical dimension testifies to the fact that both beginning and end points (and not only the end point) are implicit in the process. By means of the cyclical dimension, the process's beginning point is not lost, but, instead, becomes a party to each subsequent moment of the process. Thus, at one and the same time, the process moves forward and also collects (or gathers together) those earlier sequences in its history which it is also transcending. Because of the simultaneous retention and juxtaposition of beginning and end points, Ernst Bloch has a structural basis for declaring that the *telos* is also the *novum* and that genesis is yet to come.

In more specific terms, the principle Bloch enunciates is called metempsychosis. If salvation must be corporate (because mankind is alienated), and if the process is recapitulative, then all men, and not just a few selected men, must be brought to share in the *novum*'s largess. But since death

29. "Recapitulation" is characteristic of process-conceptualization whether the thought pattern in question be that of St. Irenaeus (who expressly speaks of "recapitulation" in his *Adversus Haereses*, particularly in Book III of that work), Teilhard de Chardin (see, for example, his *The Phenomenon of Man* [New York: Harper and Row, 1959], esp. p. 294), or Alfred North Whitehead who, in *The Aims of Education* (New York: Macmillan Company, 1929), argues that the romance-precision-generalisation rhythm of education is both perpetual and repetitive.

is a reality, and not mere appearance, all men must be restored eventually if the commonwealth of freedom is to truly be. This requires, more specifically, a transmigration of souls. Bloch argues that "if the Last Day is to define the number of souls, the number of souls also defines the Last Day."[30] Then he goes on to say that the function of the idea of metempsychosis is to insure the eventual maturation of the race.

> According to the . . . idea of metempsychosis, . . . the mere number of souls has long been complete; what is still missing and therefore, of course, poses problems more profound than those of quantity, is the *maturity* of souls; this alone will determine the end.[31]

Metempsychosis functions, then, to make certain that development, growth, and maturation are characteristic of the process. It is the content attributed to recapitulation. The achieved *telos* must be qualitatively superior to any of the antecedent points in the succession.

> The rule would then be: nothing in life is singular; no accident is irrevocable; the five foolish virgins could find oil even after midnight; the *status viae* extends far beyond death. . . . Thus the last things, which we feared we would not see, are also coming very close to us as we live over and over. We must set the switches; we bear the agony of setting the course; but at the same time, we go along. As ourselves, not merely remembered, we go the good, living way, the way of the goal; we follow it to the end because we *are* the way.[32]

The goal can be reached because "we make several appearances," each of which holds the possibility of bringing improvement. "Not at all times, but intermittently—and above all at its end—we live the entire life, the broad,

30. Bloch, "Karl Marx, Death and the Apocalypse," p. 50.
31. Ibid.
32. Ibid., p. 57.

historical life that is assigned to 'mankind' as a whole."[33] Thus, the voyage goes on, even after individual death, and the reality of every man extends far beyond the particularities of any one of his given existences. In this recapitulative repetition of life, lies "the ability to work on our real 'son of man'." What an individual could not effect in "a single lifetime"—the very thought of a single life is inconceivable to Bloch—is open to corporate man and recurrent men. And the eventual realization of *telos* depends upon the increase of quality as well as the maintenance of numerical strength:

> Everything could pass away, but the house of mankind must keep its full numerical strength and must stand lighted, so that some day, when the holocaust rages outside, we can be helped by the human achievements that inhabit it; and it is precisely from metempsychosis that such thinking leads to the point of genuine social, historical, and cultural ideology. . . .[34]

Bloch makes the same point in a slightly different way in speaking about the necessity of metempsychosis:

> And . . . above the history which we can keep repeating and around whose meanings we can play, metempsychosis simultaneously arranges for the presence, the tested presence, of all subjects at the *end* of history. It guarantees the concept of "mankind" in its absolute entity, in its then quite concretely complete numerical strength.[35]

Then, in speaking about the final age, the end of history, Bloch mixes holocaustic, apocalyptic language with the familiar water imagery:

> The waters pour off; earth's fiery flow is extinguished; even the great mutations of the organic world have lost their strength—but men have stayed at work, and now it is they

33. Ibid.
34. Ibid., pp. 57–58.
35. Ibid., p. 58.

who will finish the broad, historical subjective metaphysics: the life of time (which overtakes all as it thunders against the heavens), and of its restless exemplification in the name of God.[36]

This is the realization of utopia. Feuerbach's potentially perfect individual God-man has been replaced by qualitatively finished mankind, and all prior potential supermen have given way to corporate man. And that man, through the process, has indulged in a series of progressively more effective self-encounters.

Thus, the revolutionary principle has been exercised. The Marxist framework has been revised, though not left behind. The fundamental principles of a horizontally formed thought model have been adhered to. And place has been given to such phenomena as dreams, imagination, fantasy, and mystery. At the same time, Bloch did not have to surrender his intention of supplying a practical philosophy or a program of specific action. He can tell men what they ought to do, and he can also show them their place within the larger scheme of things. Along the way, hardly any topic—politics, literature, art, religion, science, classical mythology, folklore, astronomy, cosmology, mysticism, et al.—goes by untouched. Eventually, they all feed into the process by which the fundamental human urge is given expression as well as satisfaction. And, as the appointed custodian of that process, and steward of its mysteries, Ernst Bloch has said that his singular goal is to help man become what man knows he must be. Man was made to hope, and he remains restless, *positively* restless,[37] until the creative cycle of human history comes to enjoy hope's fulfillments.

36. Ibid.
37. The reference to Augustinian terminology here is intentional (author's note).

THREE

Jürgen Moltmann:
Theological Proversions

> It seems to me that Christian theology of today should turn away from a dogmatic theology to a critical one, from beginning with answers about God to the unsolved asking for God. The tense of asking is the future. . . . A "theology of hope" is a theology of questions that can be answered only by the coming of God through the kingdom of his freedom.
>
> —Jürgen Moltmann

In Europe it is often said that the theology of hope is neither a school nor a movement but a book, namely, the title of Jürgen Moltmann's epoch-making book which dates whatever "movement" there is from the sixth decade of the twentieth century.[1] But a more accurate genetic account of the "hope phenomena" would place its origin farther back, at least as far back as the First World War. Its advocates often refer its origin to the centrality given to history in the Old Testament biblical tradition, and, on the philosophical side, to the fragments of the early process thinker Heraclitus. And, if its intellectual stimuli do not consciously refer back to the writings of Heraclitus, they at least find some resting point in the early writings of Karl Barth. It is not Barth's *Church Dogmatics* which are implicit here as much as his

1. Jürgen Moltmann, *Theologie der Hoffnung* (Munich: Kaiser Verlag, 1965). This book first appeared in English translation as *Theology of Hope,* trans. James W. Leitch (London: SCM Press, and New York: Harper and Row, 1967).

attitudes toward the interdependencies between the Christian religion and Western culture. As Barth saw these, especially at a time when war was pervasive, religion and culture could never become so intermixed that the objective of the one could be assumed to be the purpose of the other. If religious aspiration was to retain its vitality, it would do so only by serving its own proper sphere of operation. It could not rely on its alliance with culture, nor was much strength to be gained from its cultural investments. For the alliance with culture could only rob religious aspiration of its ability to stand in judgment over culture. When religion loses that capacity, cultural endeavor comes to make claims which border on naiveté. It makes claims regarding the possibilities of man's accomplishments which, Barth thought, are not adequately conversant with the weakness of man's nature. It speaks about human progress without full recognition of the fact, to borrow a phrase of Paul Ricoeur, that man is a "flawed creature."[2] Barth was well aware of the flaw, and he saw man's flaw dramatically pitted against man's cultural aspirations as the guns sounded signaling the beginning of World War I.

Karl Barth—like Jürgen Moltmann—lived in a world which was understood not to be harmonious. For Barth, the world was split, just as man's nature was split. And this fundamental inchoateness permeated all things, from the most social of man's acts to the most resolute of his individual aspirations. Man is split as the world is split, and both reflect the more fundamental ontological split between what is and what ought to be. The examples of that fundamental inchoateness are not simply theoretical. They are compellingly in evidence in the conflict between the various parties

2. Paul Ricoeur, *Fallible Man,* trans. Charles Kelbley (Chicago: Henry Regnery, 1965).

to the once Holy Roman Empire—an alliance, one recalls, whose formative elements included biblical faith and whose glue was an Augustinian synthesis of that faith with classical philosophy, Roman law, and natural-subjective religious tendencies. That alliance had come apart, as both Barth and Moltmann recognized, and, as a result, one could never quite feel at home in the world.

Jürgen Moltmann must have pondered these matters—if not yet precisely in these terms—in the mid-fourth decade of the twentieth century in the prisoner-of-war camp in northern Scotland, just one generation after Barth gave his assessment of a similar wartime phenomenon. And, if Jürgen Moltmann did not think it at the time, a compatriot of his was not only thinking it, but was also writing it down in a series of suggestive letters and papers from another prison.[3] Dietrich Bonhoeffer, from his prison cell, saw the breakup of the old European religio-cultural alliance, a civilization which had survived (with its fundamental ingredients spliced together in delicate arrangement) for well over a millennium and a half. As Bonhoeffer saw it, the split between "what is" and "what ought" was so profound that it affected every aspect of human life. Indeed, its influence was so extensive that even Western civilization itself was threatened. Much more soberly, because of the split, the civilization in process of breaking up could not be relied upon to piece itself together again by means of the same materials. The old Holy Roman Empire—despite Bonhoeffer's expressed love for things Roman, his devotion to things holy, and his feelings for empire—would never occur again. And, since Christendom is that empire's surrogate, it too was in process of dissolution, never again to be able to

3. Dietrich Bonhoeffer, *Letters and Papers from Prison,* ed. Eberhard Bethge (New York: Macmillan Company, 1967).

reassemble itself. Indeed, if religion was to survive the cataclysm, it would do so only at the expense of Western culture, and not by forming a partnership with it. This Dietrich Bonhoeffer saw, and the younger Jürgen Moltmann came to accept. And the diagnosis became so well accepted that in 1959, Pope John XXIII could rely on its credibility and force when he called for a time of *aggiornamento,* and announced a second Vatican Council.[4]

The announcements of the end of Christendom tended to invoke a new kind of chronicle for charting and measuring the occurrences of things religious. Had the occurrences been less dramatic and decisive, it might have been possible to refer to them in terms of the language of growth and development. But, since the announcement pertained to the termination of Christianity, that language was not altogether suitable. Termination always means cessation of continua; thus the breaking-up of Christendom could not be explained simply as a new chapter in an ongoing and more comprehensive story. Neither could it be seen as an implicit extension or elaboration of something that had occurred before. Instead of being able to maintain the events that had preceded it, it had to part company with them. Seen within the perspective of the past millennium and a half it was something new, something which fell outside that perspective and made the perspective applicable only to a bygone era. The difficulty was not caused by something that didn't quite fit the perspective, but by a perspective that no longer fit.

4. Pope John XXIII's announcement was made on January 25, 1959. It is recorded in *Acta Apostolicae Sedis* ("Acts of the Apostolic See"), the official record of papal statements, vol. 51 (1959), p. 511. Pope John's announcement of a second Vatican Council is reviewed and expanded in the apostolic constitution "Humanae Salutis," December 25, 1961, by which the Council was convocated (cf. *The Documents of Vatican II,* ed. Walter M. Abbott, S.J. [New York: America Press, 1966], pp. 703–9).

When the continuum is removed, all that is left of the language of growth and development are simply the formal words that apply to time. There is talk, for example, about the end of the age. It is said that an old age has ended, and that a new age stands beyond the threshold. If old things are to survive the transition, they will do so only after becoming renewed. Some see the old passing away, with nothing more than a void standing in readiness beyond it. In some quarters, confidence is expressed that, at last, the world has "come of age." Thus, if the world is in a new age, its religious aspirations must be tailored accordingly. Some of those aspirations will be the products of the process of renewal; others are formed by the purposes toward which renewal aspires. As Dietrich Bonhoeffer saw it, presumably, the passing of the old, as momentous and agonizing as it was, signaled the dawning of a fresh beginning point. It was more dynamic than an aging process, more dramatic than the movement from childhood to adolescence to adulthood, less dialectical than the sequence thesis-antithesis-synthesis, and more profound than the familiar pattern, magic to religion to science. The process through which the world was moving could be likened only to what happens to an embryo when its embryonic "state" has been shaken off. In limited senses, some forms of continuity are maintained. But, in other senses, what follows is not another stage in an ongoing series, but a veritable postembryonic age. This Dietrich Bonhoeffer saw transpiring in the world of the middle decades of the twentieth century. The world itself had become postembryonic.

Of course, Jürgen Moltmann's thought is no mere extension of Barth's or Bonhoeffer's impressions regarding the fate of Western culture. As a student of Western religion and intellectual history, Moltmann knows that the two chief ingredients in Bonhoeffer's appraisal of the present configuration of things, the great split between "what is" and "what ought to be," and the cataclysmic end of an age, do not belong to the twentieth century alone. Moltmann, with Bloch's help—and, certainly, had he made use of it, with the aid of such historians as Mircea Eliade, Norman Cohn, Sylvia Thrupp, and Frank E. Manuel, as well as several *Daedalus* study-committees[5]—notices that that same attitude has had proponents throughout Western history, particularly in the Middle Ages. But the place where that attitude seems to prevail more fully than anywhere else, he believes, is in the New Testament itself, which, as Ernst Käsemann has argued, is an apocalyptic book. It is an apocalyptic book because the first Christians were an apocalyptic and eschatological community. Moltmann noted this, and he seized upon the correlation. The theology of hope seems to have been born, then, when Jürgen Moltmann fashioned the instrumentation with which to tie a dominant twentieth century mood to earliest Christianity. He detected their common apocalyptic and eschatological sources. He found in the New Testament the materials by which systematic theology could be reconstructed according to the thrust of mid-twentieth century, postwar religious aspirations.

But there is more. Since Bonhoeffer's time the theological

5. See Mircea Eliade, *The Myth of the Eternal Return,* trans. Willard R. Trask (New York: Bollingen Foundation, 1954); Norman Cohn, *The Pursuit of the Millennium* (New York: Harper and Row, 1961); Sylvia Thrupp, *Millennial Dreams in Action: Essays in Comparative Study* (The Hague: Mouton, 1962); Frank E. Manuel, ed., *Utopias and Utopian Thought* (Boston: Beacon Press, 1967); "Toward the Year 2000: Work in Progress," *Daedalus,* Summer 1967; *Eranos Jahrbuch,* vol. 32 (1963); Charles L. Sanford, *The Quest for Paradise* (Urbana: University of Illinois Press, 1961); A. J. Wensinck, "The Semitic New Year and the Origin of Eschatology," in *Acta Orientala* (Lund), vol. 1 (1923), pp. 158–99; and a host of other articles referred to in the footnotes and citations of the works listed here. Of special mention are two works by Vittorio Lanternari, "Messianism: Its Historical Origin and Morphology," in *History of Religions* 2, no. 1 (1962): 52–72, and *Religions of the Oppressed* (New York: Mentor Books, 1965).

mood in Europe, and Germany in particular, has been generated in large part by conflicts between so-called Christian and Marxist ideologies. The thought of Ludwig Feuerbach looms large in that confrontation, for, in addition to giving Marx the thrust of his criticism of religion, Feuerbach also attempted a reinterpretation and reconstruction of Christianity, which, to a great extent, were prefigured by analyses very similar to those later set forth by Dietrich Bonhoeffer.[6] Thus, Feuerbach's thought has found its way into recent conversation, even though the man himself has been dead for one hundred years. According to the interpretations that Feuerbach fostered, religion is regarded as the major force in a hierarchized world to keep people in subjection, and to insure the rights, properties, and privileges of those of noble parentage, proper station, and degree. To redress those cultural and economic imbalances, a colossal reversal was called for: that which had been placed at the top of the hierarchical ladder must be submerged, and that which had been placed at the lowest levels must be placed on top. Then, instead of looking to the nobles to supply their needs, the poor must take things into their own hands, bringing down the nobles, if need be. Similarly, rather than calling upon God as the noble provider of happiness and human comfort, at some future time in some anticipated other state, the poor should insert their own dreams and

6. Though there are vast differences in their approaches and contentions, Feuerbach and Bonhoeffer do indeed cross lines at a number of key points. For example, both are critical of the kind of theistic supernaturalism which places God over man as an alien being. In that sense, both work toward a this-worldly form of religious piety. Similarly, Feuerbach's willingness to call religion "an art of life" depends upon the kind of transfer which Bonhoeffer also employs in shifting from theory to action when locating religion's base. Feuerbach's attempt to use "projection" to explain religion away is not totally unlike Bonhoeffer's reference to the deceptions implicit in "the beyond"; for Bonhoeffer, those deceptions make it necessary to work toward a "religionless Christianity." For a detailed analysis of Feuerbach's philosophy, see Eugene Kamenka, *The Philosophy of Ludwig Feuerbach* (London: Routledge and Kegan Paul, 1970).

visions, and work to realize them here and now. The reversal was appropriate because religion was simply a projection of human limitation toward a state or level at which all limitations are finally removed. As Feuerbach viewed it, religion is the practice of making extravagant projections which disguise the fact that the responsibility for meeting human need belongs corporately to mankind. "God" is just as ineffective as the nobles in providing lasting happiness. In fact to believe in either one—since the nobles use "God" to maintain their position in the hierarchy and to pacify those who are not so positioned—is to fall victim to a deception. This, Feuerbach saw, is the deception which prevents man from achieving his purpose.

There is some of Feuerbach in Moltmann, just as there is much of Feuerbach to which Moltmann takes exception.[7] But the true connection between Feuerbach and Moltmann is Ernst Bloch. As there is some of Feuerbach in Moltmann, so is there much of Feuerbach in Bloch.[8] Bloch appreciates Feuerbach in the way a contemporary (though revisionist) Marxist would respect a principal catalyst of the movement

7. In his references to Ludwig Feuerbach, Moltmann seems to be most interested in three related sets of issues: (a) Feuerbach as the source of Marxist ideology and criticism of religion (cf. Moltmann's *Umkehr zur Zukunft* [Munich: Kaiser Verlag, 1970]); (b) Feuerbach's brand of "atheistic religion" (see Moltmann's essay "Die Kategorie *Novum* in der Christlichen Theologie," in *Perspektiven der Theologie: Gesammelte Aufsätze* [Munich: Kaiser Verlag, 1968], pp. 174–88, and "Die Revolution der Freiheit," in *Perspektiven*, pp. 189–211, both of which essays appear in English translation in Jürgen Moltmann, *Religion, Revolution and the Future*, trans. M. Douglas Meeks [New York: Charles Scribner's Sons, 1969], pp. 3–18 and 63–82); and (c) Feuerbach's substitution of vertical categories with horizontal ones. In this third sense, Moltmann quotes Feuerbach with approval: "For, in the words of Ludwig Feuerbach, it [faith] puts 'in place of the beyond that lies above our grave in heaven the beyond that lies above our grave on earth, the historic *future*, the future of mankind'" (in *Theology of Hope*, p. 21).

8. Bloch's book, *Atheismus im Christentum* (Frankfurt: Suhrkamp Verlag, 1968) can indeed be regarded as a commentary on Feuerbach's philosophy of religion.

to which he belongs. And as there is much sympathy in Moltmann for oppressed peoples, so is there in Bloch an ongoing identity with those whom the hierarchy has either overlooked or undernourished. The three share the conviction that oppression is the direct result of hierarchical thinking, and that the hierarchy serves as an instrument to maintain the authority of the high-born, well-positioned, and fortunately endowed.[9] Moltmann also recognizes that Feuerbach's attitude is shared in the underground, and that the underground is the place of refuge for apocalyptic and eschatological peoples.

Moltmann, however, does not attribute belief in God to a human deception, although he would not quarrel with Feuerbach regarding the latter's attempt to unmask the hierarchical "God." He agrees with the interpretation that the hierarchical "God" is employed to support the oppression of the poor. Nevertheless, he is not willing to dispense with God, nor even to settle the question by reference to inevitable (perhaps even necessary) human projection. Moltmann will not say that God "is" or that "God is not," but he has no difficulty saying that God is "still not yet." At this point, however, Moltmann's language is Bloch's, and Feuerbach's only as it is reflected in Bloch. The God who is "still not yet" is the God who is hierarchically "powerless," the God in whom Bonhoeffer believes, not the anti-God Bonhoeffer found located beyond the borders. Thus, with some special tailoring, Bloch's conception of God can be inserted in the framework of Dietrich Bonhoeffer's analysis, where it becomes more than conception. These three—Bonhoeffer, Feuerbach, and Bloch—are implicit in Moltmann's

9. If they chose to, both Bloch and Moltmann would find much of the terminology useful in Louis Dumont, *Homo Hierarchicus: The Caste System and Its Implications* (Chicago: University of Chicago Press, 1970), though, of course, Dumont's analysis is written with very different purposes in mind.

outlook. But the greatest of them, despite Bloch, is still Bonhoeffer.[10]

Ernst Bloch is helpful to Jürgen Moltmann, then, because of the variety of ingredients he is able to contain within his philosophy of hope. He captures the mood of the apocalyptic communities, and thus has fresh insight into the New Testament. He carries forward the basic Marxist interpretation of the sources of social and political oppression, and thus continues Feuerbach's program of dehierarchization. Furthermore, he gives expression to the two fundamental characteristics of apocalyptic awareness, namely, the fundamental split in man's nature which also pervades the context within which man must live, and the belief in an impending, cataclysmic event by means of which that which ought to be will be ushered in. Bloch has not given Moltmann his outlook, but he has lent both style and material to it. Bloch could not have been the sole author of a philosophy of hope, but, because of the arresting combination of interests he is able to blend, he is the one most qualified to announce the emergence of that philosophy and to give it its name. Moltmann is the one who has turned that philosophy into a Christian theology with sanction.

As it is true that theologies are usually conceived along horizontal or vertical lines, so is it true that a given theological position usually bespeaks a certain attitude to time and history and, specifically, to the history of the church.

10. It is not often noted that Moltmann's principal work, prior to the publication of *Theologie der Hoffnung,* was a study of Dietrich Bonhoeffer's concept of "the lordship of Christ and human society," *Herrschaft Christi und Soziale Wirklichkeit Nach Dietrich Bonhoeffer* (Munich: Kaiser Verlag, 1959), included in Jürgen Moltmann and Jürgen Weissbach, *Two Studies in the Theology of Bonhoeffer,* trans. Reginald H. Fuller and Ilse Fuller (New York: Charles Scribner's Sons, 1967). One can make a good case that *Theologie der Hoffnung* is an elaboration, refinement, and extension of certain motifs either expressed or hinted at in Bonhoeffer's writings.

With respect to tradition and historical antecedents, a theologian may want to be saying something very new, or he may choose to give new expression to something which was said before. If he goes to the past, it may be a particular moment or segment of the past which he wants to keep alive. It may even be all of the past which is understood as a kind of collective testimony.

Moltmann's views are no disappointment in this respect. He is very much aware of history, and senses the importance of coming to terms with history. Furthermore, he does not claim to be devising a "new doctrine," as novel or as innovative as the theology of hope may be. He does not even wish to be particularly creative. He understands the theological position he is articulating to be an old strain in the Christian repertoire. It reaches back all the way into the New Testament, and, before that, even to the time of the prophets Jeremiah and Isaiah. And, since that time, through all succeeding generations, it has been kept alive in the underground. The apocalyptic movement has always had representatives and spokesmen.

Most of Moltmann's historical cues were provided by the great church historian of two or three generations ago, Adolf von Harnack, of the University of Berlin. As Harnack interpreted the history of the Christian church, there was a radical difference in the motivations which pervaded the first Christian communities and those which came to prevail after that initial period had come to an end. Harnack believed the difference was one of fundamental intention, and also of basic temperament. The earliest Christians had been living in the expectation of the kingdom of God; however, after generations had gone by without witnessing the realization of the kingdom, their counterparts in the third, fourth, and fifth centuries tended to give more attention to

the perpetuation of the institutional church. The sign of
that shift was the systematic interest that Christians devoted
to matters of belief, thought, and social structure. In Harnack's view, the simplicity of the Christian kerygma, the
gospel whose central feature had to do with the coming of
the kingdom of God, had eventually given way to concern
for "Christianity" (the phenomenon which occurred when
Greek thought and language forms were imposed upon
New Testament religious affirmations).[11] Harnack referred
to this process as "hellenization," a development he termed
both "inevitable" and "regrettable"—much in the spirit of
some others who have called the Reformation a "tragic
necessity."[12] But Harnack's "regrettable inevitability" was
a judgment based on a very Protestant reading of church
history. It enabled him to approach Martin Luther as the
great hero of restoration, the one sent by God to redress the
earlier mistake. In Harnack's eyes, Luther tried to reverse
the process of hellenization so as to recover the purity and
simplicity of the earlier kerygma after it had been in bondage to formal and systematic portrayal these many long

11. Adolf von Harnack's thesis is summarized in his book *What Is
Christianity?* trans. Thomas Bailey Saunders (New York: Harper and
Row, 1957). I have discussed his contention at greater length in an
article, "Harnack and Ecumenical Discussion," in *Journal of Ecumenical Studies* 3, no. 3 (1966): 486–502. Since the appearance of
my article, the question of "hellenization" has taken on new dimensions because of the new assessments of its significance by Leslie
Dewart, *The Future of Belief: Theism in a World Come of Age* (New
York: Herder and Herder, 1966), and Bernard J. F. Lonergan, "The
Dehellenization of Dogma," in *Theological Studies* 28, no. 2 (1967):
336–51. From another side, previous understanding has been challenged by Robert L. Wilken, *The Myth of Christian Beginnings* (New
York: Doubleday, 1970).

12. I first heard this phrase in a lecture given by Jaroslav Pelikan. Its
substance is articulated in Pelikan's *The Riddle of Roman Catholicism*
(New York: Abingdon Press, 1959) and *Obedient Rebels: Catholic
Substance and Protestant Principle in Luther's Reformation* (New
York: Harper and Row, 1964).

centuries. Luther was the champion of fundamental, neo-primitive Christianity.

Moltmann sees the situation in somewhat similar fashion. For him, however, there is no one historical figure who stands out as hero, but, instead, a number of heroes who have kept the truth alive through the centuries. As he is fond of saying, the vision of the first Christians did not disappear after the first community was replaced by others; it merely went underground. And it lived there; it flourished there, until today, when it has once again surfaced in very dramatic fashion.

Many of these views are expressed or hinted at in Molt-mann's so-called chronicle of the *novum*. Particularly in his address at Saint Xavier College in Chicago,[13] the author of *The Theology of Hope* traces the movement of the *novum* from the time of the Hebrew prophets who announced or declared that something new was on the horizon—a new thing which Yahweh was about to effect. The next large chapter in the chronicle of the *novum* occurs when Jesus appears and states that what the prophets had foretold has now come to pass. According to Jesus' words, the *novum* had occurred, for "there are some standing here who will not taste death until they see the kingdom of God." In the proclamation of the first Christians, the new age had come. But many problems were encountered. The theoreticians in the early church did not find it easy to reconcile the *novum* with what they already understood regarding history and tradition. A complex of interrelated questions occurred: Must the old die if the *novum* is the rule? If so, what about

13. Jürgen Moltmann, "What is 'New' in Christianity," originally published in *The Future as the Presence of Shared Hope*, ed. Maryellen Muckenhirn (New York: Sheed and Ward, 1968), and contained in Moltmann, *Religion, Revolution and the Future*, pp. 3–18. The German version is included in *Perspektiven der Theologie*, pp. 174–88.

Israel? Must a Jew give up his Jewishness to be a Christian? Can one be both Jew and Christian? Must Gentiles become Jews before professing and exercising Christian faith? Because St. Paul was both Jew and Roman citizen, he found the problem to be his own (much in the style of Erik Erikson's "cultural worker" in whom self-identity is intertwined with ethos-sensitivities). St. Paul, particularly in his Epistle to the Romans, wrestled with the problems created by the occurrence of a *novum,* and found the formula by which old and new are held together in a delicate interdependence. In Paul's writings, the old is not canceled out by the devotion given to the new, it is rather embellished and fulfilled. But in the next stage of the chronicle, Marcion did in fact separate old from new. In fact, that separation was so pronounced that Marcion also thought it necessary to propose two Gods—one, the vengeful, violent, wrathful God of Old Testament history, and the other, the true, loving, compassionate Father revealed through Jesus. According to Marcion, Jesus came to proclaim the *novum,* and this signaled the end of the former dispensation. For Marcion, Christianity was new, not a mere continuation of something old nor an extension of Israelite tradition.

Commenting on the Marcionite development, Moltmann states that it was an unfortunate incursion which the church was forced to declare heretical. But, Moltmann says, "as is always the case with the exclusion of heretics, the church became more united but it also was poorer"[14]—poorer because the exclusion of Marcion had the effect of subverting the *novum.* The *novum* did not disappear, however. Instead it went underground, there to remain, the almost exclusive motivational property of oppressed peoples (people who had no real position on the hierarchical scale) and

14. Moltmann, *Religion, Revolution and the Future,* p. 14.

apocalyptic communities (communities which believed that the split in the world could only be overcome by a cataclysmic event of God's own doing). Thus, from post-Marcion times to the present—as Jürgen Moltmann views it —there are two rival parties, as it were: the one is vertically oriented, hierarchically motivated, and institutionally structured; and the other is peopled by those who expect the end of the age to come, do not feel particularly "at home" in this world, and understand themselves, to greater and lesser degrees, to be pitted against an overpowering, overbearing, and menacingly threatening "establishment."

Through Jürgen Moltmann's integrative talents, the theology of hope is enabled to weave these several strands of historical commentary together. The Feuerbachian-based assessment of the way in which religion perpetuates poverty can be given added historical credibility by reference to Harnack's discussion of the way in which hierarchical order was imposed upon an early Christian vision. The hierarchy can be made responsible for the equation of the highest with the best, and for the supremacy of the hierarchically exalted over those of more humble status. Both Harnack and Feuerbach place the blame on the imposition of hierarchical projection, and are suspicious about its motivation. In other words, Harnack's schema can be tapped to help chronicle the events that led to the socio-religious situation Feuerbach found to be intolerable. Then Bonhoeffer, in turn, wants to announce that the situation Feuerbach found to be detestable is coming to an end. When looked at from the point of view of Harnack's interests, Bonhoeffer can be understood to be declaring that the age produced by the hellenization of the earlier kerygma is languishing in its final moments; the religious-cultural alignments implicit in its structural hierarchy are certainly breaking up. And Moltmann, care-

fully selecting the judgments of his well-chosen predecessors, can supply additional fodder. Seen from the visions of
apocalyptic religious communities, there is an agelong battle
between those who have assigned themselves to securing
permanent position, and those whose motivations come
through a *novum*. From all apparent signs, the latter communities have not fared well vis-à-vis their gentried counterparts. And yet, the state of not faring well in a world which
is not one's own is one of the distinguishing marks of
oppressed peoples. Such people have always been, but they
haven't always made themselves recognized or dramatically
visible. But that situation has changed. In Bonhoeffer's
"world come of age" there is redress of Feuerbach's grievances. And, from within the underground, an underground
from whose resourcefulness the oppressed peoples are even
now participating in an exodus, that redress is no cause for
alarm. Rather, it is a sign of hope.

Moltmann is opposed to the institutional stabilizing of
things just as Harnack believed "hellenization" to be unfortunate, and Bonhoeffer felt modified and tempered exhilara-
tion in sensing that the old religio-cultural alliances were
coming apart. It is probably not so much that institutions
or institutionalization, as Moltmann sees them, are wrong
or bad, as it is a case that history is dynamic and the world
is in motion. There is nothing wrong with the cathedral until
one discovers that it is not equipped to be a vehicle of
passage. And passage is the key—both in the world and in
the church. Furthermore, institutions serve to keep past
events and traditions alive, and to make them perpetually
functional. But the apocalyptic communities, the oppressed,
the peoples of the underground, are not motivated by past-
alive-in-the-present, but, instead, by present-yielding-to-
future. They do not feed on memory or nostalgia, but,

instead, keep a projected "ought" in view. Moltmann believes that these shifts in emphasis can be effected by changing some of the "re" words, *re*formation, *re*volution, *re*newal, *re*storation, even *re*ligion to "pro" words, *pro*-formation, *pro*-volution, *pro*-newal, *pro*-storation, and even *pro*-ligion.[15] The point is obvious. The words which imply keeping the past alive in the present should be transposed into words directed toward enlivening the future. "Pro" does that, by counteracting the regressive character of "re." And "pro" is the proper prefix since the world itself is in motion, and is being pulled toward the future. Within this context, the church's main function, as Moltmann sees it, is to challenge the status quo so that life can be kept flowing and free.[16] The church is the ship, the vessel made fit for a rite of passage.

To place the thought of Jürgen Moltmann within the framework of Western religious intellectual history is not to suggest that he would be content to leave it there. He is not an intellectual historian, nor even a surveyor of apocalyptic movements. Instead, as theologian, he is also something of a social prophet, albeit a tempered, cautious one. Thus, his writings consist not only of theological statements, systematically or consistently ordered. But, at least by inference or implication, they set forth a program of social action and cultural work.

For example, in noting that the church should be likened to an ark, or ship, Moltmann looks upon the function of the church as being both critical and revolutionary. The function of the church is to prevent any institutional stabilizing of things. It is to be the vanguard of future movement. It is

15. See Moltmann, "Religion, Revolution and the Future," in *Religion, Revolution and the Future*, pp. 19–41.
16. Significantly, Moltmann entitles the chapter on the church in *Theology of Hope*, "Exodus Church."

to ride atop change, and, also, to form or guide change. The church is the instrument of the exodus, the vehicle by means of which transformaion of the status quo is effected.

Similarly, when he turns to the New Testament, and more specifically to the meaning of the kerygma he does so under the rubric of a "political hermeneutic."[17] He seizes upon the word "protest" in this regard, and then declares that the gospel of the early Christian community was not an *opium* for suffering people, but a protestation against real affliction. The cross is a confirmation of the reality of suffering against which the resurrection is an event of protest:

> When we understand the cross of Christ in this connection as an expression of real human affliction, then the resurrection of Christ achieves the significance of the true "protest" against human affliction. Consequently, the missionary proclamation of the cross of the Resurrected One is not an opium of the people which intoxicates and incapacitates, but the ferment of new freedom. It leads to the awakening of that revolt which, in the "power of the resurrection" (as Paul expresses it), follows the categorical imperative to overthrow all conditions in which man is a being who labors and is heavily laden.[18]

Protest is necessary, in Moltmann's view, because of man's bondage in the world.

The point at issue, in this respect, is the question about the currency and present applicability of biblical statements. If biblical statements are simply theoretical, then a hermeneutic which recovers an undersanding of the past would be sufficient. But this would be a hermeneutic which works retrospectively, and, of course, would be unsatisfactory to Moltmann for the very reasons he already gave in wanting

17. Cf. Jürgen Moltmann, "Toward a Political Hermeneutic of the Gospel," in *Union Seminary Quarterly Review* 23, no. 4 (1968): 303–23, republished in *Religion, Revolution and the Future,* pp. 83–107.
18. Ibid., pp. 313–14.

to change "re" words to "pro" words. The hermeneutic which is valid is the one which is also practicable. And that one must be *pro*-spective rather than *retro*-spective; it must inspire action instead of being lodged in theory; and it must treat the present in the light of the future rather than simply coming to terms with the past. The biblical statements must come to serve men as they protest against the present time of affliction, by the expectation and inspiration of the coming kingdom of God.

When it is all said, and the gifted Tübingen theologian has articulated biblical motifs in light of a future which men sometimes both fear and mistrust, the stresses which seem most prominent are those which belong to the apocalyptic mode. There are the familiar references to pervasive present affliction, impending catastrophic and sweeping changes that will affect the very fiber of social and cultural life, and the dawning age in which the protests against the present life and its multiple inequities have given way to doxology. Then, too, there is the constant reminder that man lives in a world split between "is" and "ought," because man himself is afflicted with the same fundamental dichotomy. As suggested earlier, this split is manifested in many ways and on a variety of levels. Indeed, its pervasiveness comes to imply that the world itself lacks harmony. In metaphysical terms, the slogan would read that "reality and truth *are not* one." This would mean that manifest discrepancies written into the heart of things are so real and prevalent that they tend to become reality's norm. Reality itself—whatever that term really means—is split. It is inchoate, disharmonious, and extensively differentiable. Thus, it is not enough for the religious man to harmoniously relate himself to the world. Similarly, there is no way for him to find sufficiency simply in being aware of the world or in gaining insight into its unity. There is no unity yet. And whatever rhyme arranges things does not yield to perception—even gifted, extraordinary perception. If it did, it would be enough for a man to locate "the center," and to organize his affairs by means of it. But there is no abiding center in a bifurcated world. Instead, there is only awareness of the pervasiveness of a deep gulf, recognition that the gulf is not overcome by awareness, and *an abiding hope*. These attitudes are implicit in Moltmann's distinction between theoretical and actional modes, a distinction to which Dietrich Bonhoeffer devoted much attention, as well as Moltmann's "Catholic brother," Johannes B. Metz. The same set of attitudes must also have been reinforced by the prison experience, especially if that experience sensitizes one to the bondage which all men share.

And, yet, hope has to do with the eventual cessation of bondage, and an anticipated overcoming of the deep-seated gulf between "what is" and "what ought to be." This surely must be the reason Moltmann returns again and again—with almost predictable frequency—to dominant christological themes, and, more specifically, to the necessity and reality of the cross.[19] Short of the cross, there is no spanning of the world's and man's fundamental divisiveness. Apart from the cross, all human efforts at "protest"—as appropriate as they may be—lack realism. For the cross stands as the deepest visible penetration into the dynamics of realistic hope, for it accurately reflects the agony of man's situation in the world and the surety of his vindica-

19. The stress on the cross in Moltmann's more recent writings is illustrated in his essay "Politische Theologie des Kreuzes," in *Umkehr zur Zukunft*, pp. 181–87 and more especially his essay, "Theologische Kritik der Politischen Religion," in *Kirche im Prozess der Aufklärung: Essays by Johann Baptist Metz, Jürgen Moltmann, and Willi Oelmüller* (Munich: Kaiser Verlag, 1970), pp. 11–51.

tion. The cross signifies that man's fundamental divisiveness is, in some sense, also God's.

Thus, the theology of hope is almost ineluctably a theology of the cross, a theology of suffering, not because Moltmann would want it that way necessarily, but, because of the reality of human affliction and the present state of creation. It isn't simply the case that the world is not yet finished; it is also under subjection. Moltmann turns again and again to St. Paul's eighth chapter of the Epistle to the Romans where the creation is pictured as groaning in travail, awaiting the time of its adoption, having been subjected by the Creator in hope, a hope which is attached to something not yet seen. Only in the future made visible through the cross shall creation itself be free and human history fulfilled.

FOUR

Johannes Metz:
From *Praeambula Fidei*
to *Praxis*

A new relation between theory and practice, between knowing and acting, between reflection and revolution will have
to be worked out, and it will have to determine theological
thought, if theological thought is not to be left at a pre-
critical stage.
—Johannes Baptist Metz

If the second *Vaticanum* hadn't happened, Fr. Johannes
Baptist Metz might still be engaged in resolving dilemmas
placed before Thomistic epistemology by Enlightenment
philosophy. Instead, because of Vatican II, Metz has been
allowed to spend the bulk of his energies steering the
theological enterprise away from epistemological and
toward political concerns. On the surface, these two strands
seem to run in different directions. Because they do, it is
appropriate to differentiate the earlier from the more recent
thought of Johannes Metz. The former Metz had been proclaimed as one of the most articulate of Karl Rahner's students; the new Metz seems to be speaking another language.
Yet, beneath the surface, the two strands may not be divergent at all, but, rather, sequential moments on an ongoing
continuum. It is this prospect which we shall entertain in
the present chapter.

Placed historically, Metz's thought takes its origin from the nest of problems associated with the critical philosophy of Immanuel Kant. By asking the question "How is knowledge possible?" Kant had forced the demand of legitimacy upon all forms of reflection, and not least of all theology. Because of Kant, the theological enterprise was pushed into a kind of critical self-consciousness. Its confidence was badly shaken. Indeed, its very survival was at stake. Though Metz is in no sense a Barthian, he would no doubt quickly agree with Barth's judgment that Immanuel Kant

> stands by himself . . . a stumbling-block and rock of offence also in the new age, someone determinedly pursuing his own course, more feared than loved, a prophet whom almost everyone even among those who wanted to go forward with him had first to re-interpret before they could do anything with him.[1]

Thus, ever since Kant, theologians have been involved in an attempt to pick up the pieces of a once composite but now shattered outlook on the world. More precisely, ever since Immanuel Kant "denied knowledge in order to make room for faith," the Christian theological enterprise has been pointed toward the job of reconstruction. The knowledge Kant denied has been set as the object of theological recovery, hopefully, of course, without nullifying Kant's religious gains.

As I have argued elsewhere, it seems that many of the theologians' efforts in this regard have been misplaced.[2] Instead of understanding that Kant's critiques were directed toward a description—or, in current parlance, a morphology

1. Karl Barth, *From Rousseau to Ritschl*, trans. Brian Cozens (London: SCM Press, 1959), p. 150.

2. Walter H. Capps, "A Via Positiva in Kant," in *The Journal of Religion* 48, no. 4 (1968): 351–75.

—of the cognitive process, many of them took Kant to be cataloging the defensible components of the world. Under these terms, Kant's work was devastating to the theological enterprise, for it failed to uncover or secure the realities ("God, freedom, and immortality" in Kant's words) which orthodox theology finds necessary. Thus, ever since Kant, each new generation of well-intentioned theological reconstructionists has deployed many of its best talents and its ablest men to augment Kant's catalog. Kant himself found a way out (if, indeed, that is what it should be called) by drawing upon a moral base for the postulation of "God, freedom, and immortality" after demonstrating that the absence of any certifiable empirical data for the three "realities" prevented any serious cognitive case. But, through the years, Kant's recourse to the "moral" or "practical" base has satisfied only certain kinds of men. And the majority of those thinkers who are also of a "scholastic bent" have found it to be woefully deficient. At the same time, the discussion about the conditions for "God, freedom, and immortality," for all practical purposes, has been reduced to a discussion of whether or not there really is a God.

Hence, from Kant, the theological lines of response have gone in many (but almost predictable) directions. Kant wrote three great critiques, each with reference to a standard subject field. *The Critique of Pure Reason* defines, circumscribes, and describes the range of discourse of philosophy proper; *The Critique of Practical Reason* performs the same task with respect to ethics; and *The Critique of Judgment* has principal application to the field of aesthetics. As the commentators quickly noticed, each of the three can also be construed as a paradigm through which religion can also be plotted.

Thus, when the question "What is religion like?" is raised, an answer can be phrased by means of the language of at least three identifying frameworks. Religion is like or unlike philosophy, ethics, or aesthetics; it may be more like one of these than the other two; indeed, it may be so much like one of them that it is also a derivative, standing in direct dependence. Furthermore, the range of Kant's paradigmatic sketches gives the theologian a certain flexibility when he seeks to locate or specify religious interests. For example, if one cannot demonstrate the necessity for God on philosophical grounds, as Kant himself contended, he might move into the field of ethics in search of the ingredients for a much better case. Or, if neither philosophy nor ethics proved compelling, there is another subject-field (as Friedrich Schleiermacher saw) which is ripe for investigation. In this third instance, the theorist can probe aesthetic sensitivity, the categories of harmony, senses of order, indeed, subjective feeling itself, for states or conditions which might serve as reservoirs of religious belief. And the history of the theological enterprise from Kant to the present day can be told in terms of the alternating employment of these three contextual frameworks as primary reference points for locating and interpreting the subjects of both theology and religion. Each of the three frameworks has been tried and tested, and each has been subjected to expansion and refinement.

But, to be seen in proper perspective, the interest in securing theology's fundamental datum must be placed alongside another interest which figured prominently in Enlightenment thinking, namely, the question as to whether true religion is natural or revealed. If true religion is natural, then it is also public, and any man, simply by being a man, can become party to it. On the other hand, if its base is not natural, then it becomes a religion of special circumstances; and access to it is available only through revelation, tradition, a prescribed sacramental structure, an established church, and, as Søren Kierkegaard was later to say, pieces of information which are communicated to the individual from outside. Here, too, the battle lines are drawn from Kant's day to current times. Some say that anything other than the religion which is generally open to any man's natural sensibilities must be either contrived or artificial. Others say that natural propensities could never produce the great religious verities, and that religion must exhibit an other-than-human source if it is to be relied upon to lead man to salvation. Characteristically, those who defend the natural base also tend to speak of individual religious capacities, while those who side with revelation seem to have a stake in the survival of corporate groups and structural entities, whether these be apocalyptic communities, religious orders, or the holy catholic church. In the corporate sense, revealed religion comes to look very much like manifestations of "we-feeling," that is, extrapolations of the theoretical side of group identity, while in the individual sense it seems characteristically to seize upon human potentiality and to solicit man's prospects for growth and the improvement of his material conditions. Revealed religion seems to be "institutional" before it is private; natural religion relies on private experience, and seems to resist institutional ordering.

As illustrated in the book *Religion Within the Limits of Reason Alone*, Kant himself thought that one can find a natural base for the content of revealed religion. This combination, of course, enables one to have the best of both worlds. Moral imperatives are taken as the locus of religion's raison d'être. But, at the same time, those imperatives possess religious content, as one who lives under the discipline of moral imperatives comes eventually to realize. And, for Kant, the content of such moral awareness adds up to the principal tenets of the Christian faith. Moral sensitivity, in other words, is itself a kind of source of "revealed" religious truth. This fact helps confirm the validity of the Christian faith in addition to providing it with an unchallengeable sphere of applicability:

> Morality thus leads ineluctably to religion, through which it extends itself to the idea of a powerful moral Lawgiver, outside of mankind, for whose will that is the final end (of creation) which at the same time can and ought to be man's final end.[3]

As noted earlier, Kant looked upon his own efforts as being constructive rather than destructive, and positive rather than casting suspicions. In place of the hierarchical system of theology which had developed during the Middle Ages, which system, Kant argued, simply reflected the tendency of human reflection to unify its experience, he developed a religious position out of the contention that "duty is divine command." Appreciation for this position required nothing other than moral earnestness. The speculations about how the things of nature are interrelated, the attempt to use cause and effect relationships as eventual evidences of the presence of a First Cause or a Prime Mover, the entire tendency to extrapolate supernature (or the supernatural) from nature, indeed, the very assumption that the physical ingredients of the universe and the dominant interest of piety belong to a common domain—all of this was challenged by Kant's question "How is knowledge possible?" Yet, through reflecting on knowledge, via a cultivation of what can properly be called "critical reflexivity," Kant was led to a refurbishing of religious belief on moral, rather than natural-physical grounds. Furthermore, from that new natural base, he went on to show that those beliefs which Christians have revered through the ages are not canceled out when ethics give religion its fundamental datum. Nor do

3. Immanuel Kant, "Preface" to *Religion Within the Limits of Reason Alone* (New York: Harper and Row, 1960), pp. 5–6.

they become suspect when, through an increase in cognitive sophistication, reflection is turned upon reflection in order to become aware of its mechanisms, capacities, and limitations. Neither the shift from the natural-physical to the ethical base, nor the process of turning thought back upon thought dissolves or destroys the content of religious belief. Instead, Kant believed he had found a way of safeguarding religion in addition to giving a cogent rendering to fundamental Christian convictions.

But the majority of Kant's theologian-critics have not been satisfied with the outcome. Intent on giving religious aspiration a firmer foundation, and, particularly in providing stronger or more compelling reasons for belief in God, they have tinkered with the Kantian corpus, hoping to discover weaknesses in its fiber, or places in which it can be significantly expanded. As noted earlier, the most persistent of these attempts have built upon a reversion to the natural-physical base, and have included a contention that belief in God can be given a natural-physical confirmation. Then, some have gone on to argue that the natural-physical base (which contains built-in suggestions regarding the non-physical nature of God) can also be construed as support for the kind of religion exercised in communities which also honor revelation. In short, the goal of many reconstructive theological attempts after Kant has been to give credence to Christian faith by attesting to the reality of its supernatural components. The intention seems to be the recovery of the former medieval world outlook but in such refined and sophisticated form that it eludes Kant's criticism of typical religious ideation. Looked at in a slightly different way, the goal has been a recapturing of the sacred order—a world interpreted along religious lines—in the post-Enlightenment era. The reconstructionists would like to have a position which keeps God and world together in meaningful harmony even in an age which knows through its reflective techniques how such positions are composed. Johannes Metz, along with a host of others, has given himself to the cultivation of a postcritical theology, that is, a Christian theological outlook which retains the sense of things medieval in a mode which is fully aware of the Kantian and Enlightenment temper.

The same point can be highlighted if one construes the intellectual enterprise to have been involved in the designing of paradigmatic grammars. Indeed, it is not inappropriate to construe the entire intellectual era from Kant to the present as a time in which a large number of grammars were composed. Prior to Immanuel Kant, in the Scholastic era and before, the paradigmatic grammar which was relied upon was one which cataloged the ingredients of the physical and supraphysical universe. Aristotle asked the question "What sorts of things are there?" and the scheme which resulted was one in which the things-which-are were sorted out and appropriately classified. As is well known, Thomas Aquinas accepted Aristotle's "grammar" of the physical and supraphysical universe, of course, with some refinement, correction, and significant additions, and added explanations for the sorts of things that are. In the Enlightenment period, however, a new set of intellectual interests developed, and a grammar was cultivated which pertained more directly to man's mental life than to the natural-physical universe. The shift in interest is implicit in the turn from one kind of question to another. Instead of "What sorts of things are there?" Immanuel Kant asked "How is knowledge possible?" And the models which were built were not tailored to fit the worlds of nature and physics, but, instead, to accurately reflect mental or cognitive processes. Later, in the early nineteenth century, Søren Kierkegaard reached for a grammar of a similar sort, that is, a grammar of things interior rather than things exterior, and produced a comprehensive description of *subjectivity*. The ingredients in Kierkegaard's grammar were not Kant's formal categories of reason, but such subjective touchstones as fear, dread, anxiety, confidence, and hope, and were held together by an existential dialectic which places aesthetics, ethics, and two forms of religion together on a dynamic continuum. In the same century John Henry Cardinal Newman wrote *A Grammar of Assent,* a descriptive account of the acts by which men come to believe certain things. Then, the phenomenologists judged Kant's grammar to be based on abstractions of reflection, and one which really did not take account of a more primary world, namely, the world of lived-experienced or, in Edmund Husserl's word, the *Lebenswelt.*

Those scholars under whom Johnnes Metz received his training in philosophy and theology were involved in the same task of developing a grammar to explore a range of experience which Kant left relatively untouched, and which, because of that fact, puts limits on the extent to which Kant's conclusions are valid. But for Metz's instructors, Kant was criticized not because he lacked awareness of dominions of experience in addition to philosophy, ethics, and aesthetics. It wasn't simply that he had overlooked large worlds of discourse. It was rather that in dealing with the cognitive process he had failed to observe the importance of *precognitive* or *prereflective* factors in making knowledge possible. Thus, the reason Kant went to such pains to find a place for religion was that he failed to notice its presence prior to reflection. Kant made the mistake of thinking that religion was something one arrived at as an end result of a certain kind of human activity. In point of fact, it stood more as starting point; it was there from the outset; it preceded rational or discursive activity. It is precognitive rather than postreflective or meta-ethical. Hence, religion is an influence in giving form and content to man's knowledge of the world as well as appraisal to his experiences.

To cite this history of post-Kantian attempts to provide religion with strong bases in human experience, and then to engage in meaningful reconstructive theological tasks, is to refer the thought of Johannes Metz (at least in its formative stages) to the work of the Belgian thinker, Joseph Maréchal,[4] from whose work Karl Rahner also takes many of his points of departure. It is also to indicate that there are structural similarities between Metz's thought and that of such neo-scholastic thinkers as Carlos Cirne-Lima,[5] Emerich Coreth,[6] and, with much refinement, Bernard Lonergan,[7] Gerald A. McCool,[8] and Michael Novak.[9] There

4. Joseph Maréchal, *Le Point de Départ de la Métaphysique* (Paris: Desclee de Brouwer, 1927–1949). See also Maréchal's often overlooked book, *Studies in the Psychology of the Mystics* (trans. Algar Thorold [London: Burns, Oates and Washbourne, 1927]) for a host of clues regarding his epistemological disposition. In the many discussions of Maréchal's understanding of prereflective consciousness, it is not always remembered that the author of *Le Point de Départ de la Métaphysique* was also Professor of Rational and Experimental Psychology at the Jesuit Philosophical and Theological College in Louvain where he taught biology and human physiology, studied mental pathology and legal psychiatry, and directed much of his research toward clarifying such topics as "the psychology of intuition," "the concept of presence," "spatial imagination," and "hallucinatory spatialisation." It is clear that Maréchal's attitude toward both metaphysical and epistemological issues was not formed by the same sets of data as those which impressed Immanuel Kant.

5. Carlos Cirne-Lima, *Personal Faith: A Metaphysical Inquiry,* trans. G. Richard Dimler (New York: Herder and Herder, 1965).

6. Emerich Coreth, *Metaphysik: Eine methodisch-systematische Grundlegung* (Innsbruck, 1961).

7. Bernard Lonergan speaks expressly to this point in "Metaphysics as Horizon," in *Gregorianum* 44 (1963): 307–18. The article also appears in *Collection: Papers by Bernard Lonergan, S.J.,* ed. F. E. Crowe (New York: Herder and Herder, 1967), pp. 202–20.

8. Gerald A. McCool, "The Primacy of Intuition," in *Thought* 37, no. 144 (1962): 57–73.

9. Michael Novak, *Belief and Unbelief: A Philosophy of Self-Knowledge* (New York: Macmillan Company, 1965).

are large differences in the opinions of these men, together with a variety of shadings and subtleties.[10] Yet, given such variations, there is also general agreement that the cognitive process is dynamic from first to last, and that it is set in motion by the kinds of activities which are given the names "spontaneous intuition," "insight," "constituting antic-

10. In English, the following studies refer to the issues implicit in this chapter: Otto Muck, *The Transcendental Method* (New York: Herder and Herder, 1968); George A. Lindbeck, "The A Priori in St. Thomas' Theory of Knowledge," in *The Heritage of Christian Thought: Essays in Honor of Robert Lowry Calhoun* (New York: Harper and Row, 1965), pp. 41–63; George van Riet, *Thomistic Epistemology: Studies Concerning the Problem of Cognition in the Contemporary Thomistic School* (Saint Louis: B. Herder, 1963); Helen James John, *The Thomist Spectrum* (New York: Fordham University Press, 1966); and Stephen J. Reno, "Religious Belief: Continuities Between Newman and Cirne-Lima," in *The New Scholasticism* 44, no. 4 (1970): 489–514; and the works already cited. In German, the following are representative: August Brunner, *Erkenntnis theorie* (Cologne: Bachem, 1948); Walter Brugger, "Methode der Metaphysik und der Einzelwissenschaften," in *Theologie und Philosophie* 43 (1968): 1–17; Brugger, "Dynamistische Erkenntnistheorie und Gottesbeweis," in *Melanges Joseph Marechal* (Paris, 1950), vol. 2, pp. 110–20; Josef Schmucker, *Die Primären Quellen des Gottesglaubens* (Freiburg: Herder, 1967); Josef de Vries, *La Pensée et L'Etre* (Louvain: Nauwelaerts, 1962); de Vries, "Fragen zur transzendentalen Methode," in *Scholastik* 40 (1965): 389–97; de Vries, "Der Zugang zur Metaphysik: Objective oder transzendentale Methode?" in *Scholastik* 36, no. 4 (1961): 481-96; and Ludger Oeing Hanhoff, "Wesen und Formen der Abstraktion nach Thomas von Aquin," in *Philosophisches Jahrbuch* (1963), pp. 14–37, in which the views of Coreth, Lonergan, and Cirne-Lima are analyzed.

Emerich Coreth has been especially prolific; see his *Grundfragen der Hermeneutik: Ein philosophischer Beitrag* (Freiburg: Herder, 1969); "Was ist philosophische Anthropologie?" in *Zeitschrift für Katholische Theologie* 91 (1969): 252 ff.; "Hermeneutik und Metaphysik," in *Zeitschrift für Katholische Theologie* 90 (1968): 422–50; "Die Welt der Menschen als Phanomen und Problem," in *Neue Erkenntnisprobleme in Philosophie und Theologie: Festschrift for Josef de Vries* (Freiburg: Herder, 1968), pp. 39–63; and "Unmittelbarkeit und Vermittlung des Seins," in *Zeitschrift für Katholische Theologie* 92 (1970): 313–27, an article which was first prepared as a lecture to the "First International Lonergan Congress" in St. Leo, Florida, March 31 to April 3, 1970, and constitutes an answer to Lonergan's article, "Metaphysics as Horizon."

Johannes Metz's thought is linked to the discussion of above-mentioned issues, in Helmut Ogiermann, "Die Problematik der religiösen Erfahrung," in *Scholastik* 37 (1962): 481–513, and 38 (1963): 481–518.

ipation," and "immediate grasp." Indeed, Karl Rahner refers to "human knowing" as "spirit in the world."[11] Bernard Lonergan talks repeatedly about the "horizon" within which personal faith registers. Carlos Cirne-Lima uses such terms as "free decision of will," "personal acceptance," "the attitude of the total human person to the existent," "self-forgetting, unreserved approval," and "saying yes to a concrete Thou in his dignity and singularity," for example, in describing the constituting of intuition by cognitive and volitional factors.[12] In presenting Lonergan's thought in the book *The Achievement of Bernard Lonergan,* David Tracy subtitles an early chapter "The Worlds of Symbolic and Theoretic Interiorities."[13] In every instance, the tendency is the same, namely, to emphasize the dynamic nature of intellection, and, more particularly, to call attention to the nondiscursive (spontaneous and intuitive) factors upon which every cognitive enterprise depends. Then, in addition to calling for a radical expansion of the Kantian outlook, such thinkers refer their proposals to the general Scholastic vs. Enlightenment problematic. Their intention is to register the claim that a careful reading of the works of St. Thomas Aquinas will show that the author of the *Summa Theologica* was, in fact, somewhat ahead of the author of *The Critique of Pure Reason.* Unlike the critical philosopher, St. Thomas understood that intellection was dynamic, and that a series of spontaneous acts preceded the application of formal categories to empirical data. One can also argue, so these "neo-Thomist" thinkers claim, that St. Thomas also realized that belief in God was not a conclusion to which one came at

11. Karl Rahner, *Spirit in the World,* trans. William Dych (London: Sheed and Ward, 1968).

12. Cirne-Lima, *Personal Faith: A Metaphysical Inquiry.*

13. David Tracy, *The Achievement of Bernard Lonergan* (New York: Herder and Herder, 1970), pp. 45 ff.

the end of an intellectual process, but, instead, an item given precognitively. Even the celebrated "proofs for the existence of God" are understood to be "monstrations" rather than results achieved by careful discursive reasoning. Hence, God is ingredient in the formation of one's interior and theoretic "horizon." God is constitutive of the objective validity of our judgments and of our knowledge of the world. To say it more simply, God belongs to the horizon by which we apprehend the world, give it form, and interpret our experience.

Against this theoretical background—a background in which he was both thoroughly immersed and aptly trained to teach—it seems almost inconceivable that Johannes B. Metz would first come to light, as it were, as a spokesman for "political theology," and that his reputation would be based on his effectiveness in Christian-Marxist debates over essentially economic (and not epistemological) criticisms of religion. And, yet, this is exactly what has happened. Johannes Metz has come to be accepted as the foremost Catholic spokesman within the "school of hope," a school which takes its principal cues, which we have noted, from revivals of apocalyptic and eschatological motifs, Feuerbachian criticisms against basing religious values on sociocultural class distinctions, and predictions that Christendom —that great structural constellation of philosophy, theology, law, art, and piety—is in glorious danger of collapse. How does one reconcile the mood of the hope school with the interest in reconstructing a Thomistic outlook on the basis of reassessments of Kant's critical philosophy?[14]

14. Francis P. Fiorenze, who has been Metz's student, has prepared two helpful chronicles which place Metz's thought in context: "The Thought of J. B. Metz: Origin, Positions, Development," in *Philosophy Today* 10, no. 4 (1966): 247–52; and "Karl Rahner and the Kantian Problematic," in "Introduction" to Rahner's *Spirit in the World,* pp.

The reconciliation between the two (which, even now, is in process of being worked out) is hinted at in a number of Metz's writings. His remarks indicate that his recent association with the "theology of hope" is a new departure from as well as an extension of his earlier preoccupations. For example, in the foreword to the English translation of Karl Rahner's *Geist in Welt (Spirit in the World),* Metz acknowledges his dependence on Rahner and praises his teacher highly. But then he asks whether Rahner's "anthropocentrically [as opposed to being both cosmocentric and theocentric] oriented theology" should not eventually lead to a greater emphasis on history and the world. And that question merely makes the next one inevitable. In speaking about anthropocentric stresses, Metz asks: ". . . should not the transcendental theology of person and existence be translated into a type of 'political theology'?" But this question simply sets another one in motion: If the anthropocentric theology (the theology of person and existence) leads almost ineluctably to a "political theology," should it not also give great stress to eschatology? In Metz's words:

> . . . does not every anthropocentrically oriented theology which does not want to leave the world and history out of sight of operative and responsible faith flow into an eschatologically oriented theology?[15]

But, then, to provide assurances that such questions do not really overstrain the Rahnerian outlook, Metz is gentle:

xix–xlv. Though not specifically directed toward specifying Metz's place in the discussion of Rahner's reconstitution of Kantian motifs, Fiorenze's essays "Dialectical Theology and Hope," in *Heythrop Journal* 4, nos. 2–4 (1968) are also noteworthy. While Fiorenze's essays are supportive of Metz's thought, T. Mannermaa is sharply critical of Metz's interpretation of Karl Rahner, in "Eine Falsche Interpretationstradition von Karl Rahners *Hörer des Wortes?*" in *Zeitschrift für Katholische Theologie* 92 (1970): 204–9.

15. Johannes B. Metz, "Foreword" to Karl Rahner, *Spirit in the World,* p. xviii.

"Such questions, coming out of Rahner's program, need not be solved against him, but rather can be tested and further developed in dialogue with him."[16] In his final statement of praise, Metz calls attention to Rahner's great twofold achievement in underscoring "the mystery of God's love and the service of the hope of all men."[17] Just as a great number of his predecessor teachers had met Kantian criticisms of Scholasticism by drawing upon the writings of St. Thomas to go beyond Kant, so Metz effectively employs Rahner's statements to find a way beyond Rahner. In this way, one is enabled to cross the threshold by means of protective, sanctioned aid.

Metz's break with Rahner became more visible and obvious to onlookers at the Saint Xavier College (Chicago) Symposium on "The Theological Task Confronting the Church Today" in the first week of April, 1966. In giving preface to a lecture on "The Church and the World," Metz made direct reference to the word "horizon," citing one of Karl Rahner's essays as a point of reference. But then he specified that the "horizon" through which he wants to explore the relations of the Christian to the world is the "horizon of the future."[18] This new formulation of "horizon" entailed the singling out of a particular time tense rather than a precognitive epistemological factor. In describing that horizon more fully, referring it to a series of equations (the world as history, history as final history, faith as hope, and theology as eschatology—all characteristic hope-school themes), Metz details an additional advantage:

16. Ibid.
17. Ibid.
18. Johannes B. Metz, "The Church and the World," in *The Word in History,* ed. T. Patrick Burke (New York: Sheed and Ward, 1966), p. 70.

> This horizon characterizes the attempt of theology to surpass and go beyond the modern transcendental, personalistic, and existential theology without disregarding its valuable insight.[19]

Those valuable insights have to do with giving due emphasis to personhood, finding and stressing human existence, and coming to terms with subjectivity. All of this, of course, is placed in contrast to the calculated objectivity of Scholasticism. Then, after praising that which Rahner championed, Metz goes on to underscore the limits of this implicit neo-Thomist view. It is vulnerable, in the first case, because it recognizes the *present* only, and omits the future. Secondly, its stress on the human person, human existence, and subjectivity leads to a kind of privatization and individualizing of religion. As a result, it tends to neglect the socio-political world. Metz wants to go beyond the "transcendental, personalistic, and existential" position of his teachers, to whom he remains both obligated and devoted, in much the same way that he understands them to have gone beyond a more traditional Scholastic position. He wants to do this without overhauling all that his predecessors have set forth. Indeed, with those safeguards in mind, he focuses on areas of neglect, omission, or understress, and then states that the positions he is setting forth can treat the reality of the socio-political world more effectively and can also make good use of the future tense. The break with Rahner is not at all complete—Metz would still prefer to call it an extension of his teacher's insights—and yet it was clear to Metz's hearers that the dependence which remained was more chronological than genetic. Johannes Metz had moved into a new range of discourse, and the transition was real.

From that time on, with increasing frequency and sustained interest, Metz has been saying much about the

19. Ibid.

orientation of the present world to the future. He has given much attention to modern man's inability to conceive of salvation as being something "*above* him," as it were, rather than understanding it more realistically, to be out in front of him as a prospect for mankind's good. Heaven and hell, he has said repeatedly, are real possibilities, not simply the upper and lower extensions of some untenable, mythological hierarchical order. He has also continued his efforts to convince his readers and hearers that the world as it is now is neither sufficient nor complete; and, in arguing this point, he gives much credence to the Marxist view that an active, operative, even revolutionary orientation to the future is necessary if that better world is to be accomplished. He believes, further, that the Christian faith belongs to this context, that all of it must be recast with sensitivity to this context, and that current biblical scholarship confirms the primacy of this contextual framework. With this background, after making many forays into biblical materials, Metz outlines his "creative, militant eschatology" in terms of the ways in which Christian hope is formative in building the promised city of God. As he says over and again, the realization of the vision of hope is dependent upon an alleviation of oppressive social conditions. Even if it be future-oriented, salvation can never be understood purely as an individual matter, as though it would be enough to rescue the individual from an adverse plight. Instead, salvation, properly conceived, has reference to the realization of justice in society and peace throughout the world. Justice and peace, then, are not merely concomitants of man's salvation, but are the goal and product of effective eschatological conscientiousness.

With striking frequency, Metz has also seized upon a theme made prominent in Dietrich Bonhoeffer's writings, particularly in his early work *Act and Being*,[20] namely, the distinction between theory and action. Bonhoeffer uses the distinction to argue that the norm for the Christian, the point from which he takes his orientation, is actional rather than theoretical. What makes a Christian, in more precise terms, is a "style of life" rather than something cognitive, mental, or intellectual. Metz employs Bonhoeffer's distinction most directly when speaking about foreknowledge of the future. His contention runs as follows: man (and, even more so, the Christian) has little reliable theory which can be used to anticipate the future; but there is another sort of awareness which is implicit in brotherly love. This love, which works according to the biblical pattern "We know that we have passed out of death into life, because we love the brethren" (1 John 3:14), has a sensitivity to things future which is possible to no other stance. Hence, as opposed to the Marxist who can claim an ongoing dialectical process as the source and guarantee of his information about the future, the Christian admits to a paucity of (theoretical) knowledge in lieu of what he comes to know of the future through his love of the brethren.[21] The careful reader will notice, once again, that nondiscursive modes of awareness have preceded the discursive mode. Metz finds this realignment of priorities in keeping with his intention to make the future the horizon.

The question forces itself: Is Johannes Metz one or two? Is his later thought essentially different from his earlier

20. Dietrich Bonhoeffer, *Act and Being*, trans. Bernard Noble (New York: Harper and Row, 1962).

21. Metz returns to this theme again and again. See, for example, the following essays: "Creative Hope," in *Cross Currents* 17, no. 2 (1967): 171–79; "Die Zukunft des Glaubens in einer hominisierten Welt," in *Weltverständnis im Glauben*, ed. Metz (Mainz, 1966), pp. 45–62; and "Verantwortung der Hoffnung," in *Stimmen der Zeit* 177, no. 6 (1966): 451–62, translated as "The Responsibility of Hope," in *Philosophy Today* 10, no. 4 (1966): 280–88.

thought? Is his a radical shift from a precognitive rational base for religious belief—particularly belief in God—to a thorough recognition of the reality of the secular world? Or is it of only limited consequence? Metz himself understands the new Metz to be an extension of the earlier Metz, and, in his own terms, a corrective against certain large oversights. As he portrays it, his work is essentially the kind of self-criticism which belongs within the Rahnerian school. However, some who hear him think that his criticisms carry him down a different path from Rahner's. And yet it may also be the case that the more recent Metz has found a better way to resolve the dilemmas which were the preoccupation of the earlier Metz.

When one places two of Metz's major works, *Christliche Anthropozentrik*[22] and *Zur Theologie der Welt,*[23] side by side, he can detect a very clear three-stage evolution of thought. Indeed, each of the three stages can also be understood as implicit horizons through whose perspectives Christian belief and self-understanding are registered. The starting point is the cosmocentric thought-form (*Denkform*) of the Greeks, which is the initial intellectual horizon, primarily because of its ability to separate things natural from things supernatural. In treating this horizon in *Christliche Anthropozentrik*, Metz argues that St. Thomas Aquinas was severely critical of it. Thomas's alternative—stage two!

22. Johannes B. Metz, *Christliche Anthropozentrik* (Munich: Kösel Verlag, 1962). This book is perceptively reviewed by Manfried Zahn, in *Zeitschrift für Katholische Theologie* 87 (1965): 104–8.

23. Johannes B. Metz, *Zur Theologie der Welt* (Mainz: Matthias-Grünewald, 1968), in English, *Theology of the World,* trans. William Glen-Doepel (New York: Herder and Herder, 1969). It is significant that the evolution of thought from epistemological and metaphysical issues toward the development of a kind of "theology of the world" is not unlike the progression of thought that is reflected in Emerich Coreth's writings. Two of Coreth's most recent writings have dealt with the topics of "Die Welt der Menschen" and "philosophische Anthropologie." Both can be taken as attempts to understand man apart from theological and philosophical pre-constructs.

—was an anthropocentric thought-form, a horizon which gave due place to personhood, subjectivity, and history in ways not possible cosmocentrically. As noted earlier, Thomas's great breakthrough in moving from *cosmos* to *anthropos* is also the point of Karl Rahner's innovations and, more generally, is mirrored in Enlightenment tendencies. As noted earlier too, it is through a detailed exploration of anthropocentrism (namely human personhood, subjectivity, and, finally, interiority) that a precognitive horizon is distinguished for religious belief and affirmation. And this, in turn, enables the basic Thomistic standpoint to survive the shift from cosmocentrism to anthropocentrism, and, furthermore, to serve as a resolver of fundamental dilemmas in the new Enlightenment framework. Stage three occurs when Metz departs from Rahner (as well as the large school of Maréchalian-inspired thinkers), and includes a maximization of anthropocentrism, a stressing of human history vis-à-vis personal subjectivity, and, most characteristically, a shift from present to future tense. The transition is also registered in the titles of the books. The bulk of *Christliche Anthropozentrik* (the manual of stage two) was written prior to Vatican Council II, and was published in 1962. Prior to that, Metz was filling in and filling out the Rahnerian corpus as expressed in *Geist in Welt,* the textbook of stage one. The product of Vatican II thinking, *Zur Theologie der Welt* (the programmatic of stage three), which takes many of its stresses from the Vatican II schema *Gaudium et Spes,*[24] was published in 1968. Assuming cos-

24. Cf. "Pastoral Constitution on the Church in the Modern World (*Gaudium et Spes*)," in *The Documents of Vatican II,* ed. Walter M. Abbott, S.J. (New York: America Press, 1966), pp. 199–308. Cf. Alois Grillmeier, "Kirche und Welt," in *Theologie und Philosophie* 43 (1968): 18–34, in which reference to Metz's work is made. Grillmeier's article gives a good sense of the context to which Metz has addressed his remarks, a context which includes contributions by J. Ratzinger, Y. Congar, E. Schillebeeckx, and Karl Rahner.

mocentrism to be the fundamental point of departure, and not really one of the segments of the élan, the three stages really become two. Both are anthropocentric, but the second focuses on corporate (rather than individual) issues, and saves its finest creative talents not for an unraveling of the inner dynamism of cognitive acts but to approach man's frightful future with the full resourcefulness of the Christian faith.

The substance of *Zur Theologie der Welt* is an essay which was the theme of Johannes Metz's lecture tour in the United States in the spring of 1968, "Religion and Society in Light of a Political Theology."[25] In this essay, Metz provides only a partial summary of the background from which he approaches the problem of formulating "the Christian eschatological message under the conditions and within the circumstances of present-day society." And yet he does make specific reference to the Enlightenment, and to the way in which religion was understood there. He acknowledges that, for the first time, religion came to register in socio-political terms. This was an improvement upon its earlier raison d'être, which, in the Middle Ages, derived from metaphysical considerations and depended upon a unified cosmocentric world outlook. At the same time, the new socio-political setting in a disharmonious, anthropocentric world also led to religion's undoing. Instead of confronting the socio-political environment in a critical way, religious aspirations were turned inward. Faith was privatized. The gospel came to register only in what Metz refers to as "the sphere of the person." Consequently, the reconstructive opportunity provided by the Enlightenment was missed. As Metz sees it, the theology of the time "did not pass through the Enlight-

25. This essay, "Religion and Society in Light of a Political Theology," was also published in *The Future of Hope*, ed. Walter H. Capps (Philadelphia: Fortress Press, 1970), pp. 136–54.

enment, but jumped over it and thought thus to be done with it." It became intimate, private, interior, and, by implication, apolitical. Speaking of the fashioners of this apolitical position (which, by this time, include Metz's instructors as well as the writers who responded to Enlightenment tendencies earlier), Metz writes:

> To be sure, these theologians strongly emphasize charity and all that belongs to the field of interpersonal relations. Yet, from the onset, as though there were no question, they understand charity to be nothing more than a private virtue without political relevance. It is a virtue of the I-Thou relation projected onto the field of interpersonal encounter, or, at most, extended to include the neighborhood. The category of encounter is predominant. The proper religious form of speaking is the interpersonal address. The proper dimension of religious experience is free subjectivity. From start to finish, the individual is the indispensable factor, the silent center of the I-Thou relation.[26]

Then, so that there is no doubt about whom he is vying against, Metz identifies his adversaries in the following terms: "It seems clear then that the transcendental existential and personality theology (both of which positions remain current and strong) have one thing in common, namely, the tendency to be ruled by the private."[27] Stage three has clearly emerged out of stage two after acknowledging that the anthropocentric tendencies of stage two were an inevitable and propitious supersedence of the former cosmocentrism. As Metz must view it, St. Thomas effected the first major shift, a shift which was both sustained and reinforced by Karl Rahner and the Maréchalian outlook. But, while Rahner gives a certain preview of an

26. Ibid., pp. 138–39.
27. Ibid., p. 139.

extended, deprivatized anthropocentrism—extension is made necessary by Rahner's own innovative tendencies—it is left to Johannes Metz to actually take the remedial step. Then, after taking it, in order to show that the step was both proper and inevitable, he returns to the Enlightenment problematic, claiming that the necessity for it was implicit there.

The conclusion which one must draw from this becomes quite obvious. Political theology is really the only effective postcritical resolution of the obstacles placed in the way of Christian belief by Immanuel Kant's reflexive turn. Metz can see it in no other terms. In his view, the Enlightenment strictures against religious belief must be sustained whenever it is assumed that the affirmations of faith can be deduced from a systematic delineation of the components of nature or the cosmos. Even St. Thomas Aquinas, prior to the Enlightenment, was ahead of those who adhered to a cosmocentric view. But the dilemmas are not resolved simply by a turn toward subjectivity.

As history testifies, this move tends to "privatize" religion at the expense of ascribing reality and devoting seriousness to the worlds of history and socio-political interchange. The development of a proper postcritical theology is the development of a "socio-critical theology," Metz argues, and this would be a position which constantly judges the present socio-political situation in the light of an anticipated eschatological reality. Instead of answering hard-nosed Enlightenment criticism of religion with innovative stances which attempt to elude criticism, as, for example, the development of precognitive categories attempted to do, Christian theologians should articulate the faith in critical terms. This involves, as Metz sees it, a recasting of the faith in a socio-critical thought-form. A socio-critical thought-form is one in which an eschatological critique of present conditions in society registers.

Against this background, the paramount task of the church becomes obvious. Instead of being a haven for those who are cultivating personal salvation strategies, the church should serve as the agency which carries out the necessary (and liberating) criticisms against present-day society. The church becomes a critical institution, that is, an institution which exercises criticism. It is a socio-critical institution, that is, an institution which carries out criticism against social powers and political institutions. And the church is able to engage in this task, so Metz believes, because it has no particular social ideology of its own which it is also fostering:

> In the pluralistic society, it cannot be the socio-critical attitude of the church to proclaim one positive societal order as an absolute norm. It can only consist in announcing in and to this society the message of a critical, liberating content. The church's task here is not the elaboration of a system of social doctrine, but of social criticism. The church is a particular institution in society, yet presents a universal claim. If this claim is not to be an ideology, it can only be formulated and urged as *criticism*.[28]

Consequently, because the church is not setting forth its own ideology but is only engaging in *criticism*, it is, if only in this sense, somewhat above criticism. To be sure, Metz believes that criticism must also be exercised within the church so that ecclesiastical authorities do not overstep the boundaries of their competence. In that sense the church needs self-criticism. But in the sense that an institution solely engaged in criticism cannot be criticized for carrying out anything other than a critical function, the church has become an agent rather than an object of criticism. As the

28. Ibid., pp. 152–53.

purveyor of one of the world's comprehensive ideologies, the church would fall victim to the same criticisms which are leveled against all ideologically derived institutions (whether these be cosmocentrically or anthropocentrically ordered). But if the church is not that, if it has successfully made the transition through the stages to corporate anthropocentrism, it is not vulnerable in that respect. Rather, it is in a position to carry out the socio-political task as no other living institution is equipped to do.

Thus Metz has carried out his objectives. He has clarified the Enlightenment dilemma, he believes, and he has found a way to bring the church into the mid-twentieth century as a significant socio-political force. He has done both, one can observe, by cultivating and extending Dietrich Bonhoeffer's distinction between theory and action. To understand the church as a socio-political force instead of as an ideological superstructure is to refer it to normative critical action and to make secondary its dependence upon theoretical considerations. To align the faith with action and practice vis-à-vis ideology is to make its thought-forms dynamic and perpetually innovative. And, finally, to carry out this reconstructive task is to mediate Enlightenment criticisms by acknowledging their validity. The earlier and the later Metz are, in this sense, one and the same. Both work under the constant awareness that the Enlightenment challenge to theology must be met even at the risk of sacrificing the entire enterprise. Johannes Baptist Metz, from start through *Zur Theologie der Welt,* understood Immanuel Kant to be the one to whom he must inevitably give an answer. Finally, Metz (like Kant before him) made room for practice by keeping intellection within strict limits. And, in a curious sort of way, the transition from cosmocentrism to anthropocentrism leads back again to the second of Kant's major critical works, *The Critique of Practical Reason.*[29] But, in Metz's case, all one gets is the prolegomena to that critique.

A number of critical questions are raised. Metz is fond of formal-material distinctions; he gives great stress to them in his *Christliche Anthropozentrik.* In this light, one must simply ask if Enlightenment criticism of religion can be effectively met by recourse to formal innovations. What Metz has done, it seems, is to incorporate "critique" within the Christian outlook; indeed, one might almost say that "critique" is the fundamental qualifier of the Christian attitude. The end result of his efforts is a recasting of the faith in a critical mode. Thus, the content of the faith is hardly anything more than an articulation of that mode in religious terms. Metz's resolution of Enlightenment dilemmas, then, is a modal shift. Just as Kant shifted from an ideological (or theoretical) mode to a critical one, a shift we have referred to as a "reflexive turn," so also has Johannes Metz, and with him, if his recommendations are carried out, Christian theology. Metz has attempted to match Kant's breakthrough with a reflexive turn of his own.

But Kant's point was not simply to recommend criticism or even to advocate a modal shift. He exercised both, as noted above, in order to prepare a unique kind of grammar. And, a grammar is nothing more or less than a methodical representation of the rules which govern the interrelationships between the components of specific linguistic forms. As a number of recent phenomenologists have demonstrated, grammars can also be written with respect to the

29. In this connection, it is significant that Ernst Bloch's criticism of Marxism is that it is "near to being a *Critique of Pure Reason* for which no *Critique of Pratical Reason* has yet been written" (Bloch, "Karl Marx, der Tod und die Apokalypse," in *Geist der Utopie* [Frankfurt: Suhrkamp Verlag, 1964], pp. 304–5, translated in *Man On His Own,* trans. E. B. Ashton [New York: Herder and Herder, 1970], p. 39).

rules of social interdependency; that is to say, they need not be restricted to linguistic expressions, even though, in every case, they build upon forms of symbolization. In writing his grammars, Kant thought that he had given methodical representation to the world of human symbolization—the world studied within the fields of philosophy, ethics, and aesthetics. Kant also noted that the preparation of a grammar required a particular kind of intellectual activity. Instead of simply employing the rules of logical and syntactical consistency, as one does, for example, when he learns to use a language accurately and effectively, one had to catch such consistency in the dynamism of its intrinsic act. This effort at "thinking about thinking," or mapping reflection, has already been referred to as "the reflexive turn."[30] And, to this point, criticism of Kant is appropriate in principle: As Maréchal and the other neo-Thomists see it, Kant's "grammar" had failed to take proper cognizance of the dynamism of precognitive factors in the intellective act.

In writing his grammar, Kant noted that several diverse kinds of ingredients were necessary to consistent intellection, one of which he called "the formal categories" and another of which he termed "principles." In delineating these formal components, he was also engaged in an effort to circumscribe the range over which his succession of grammars were applicable. And, in turn, he took each one of them, and delimited its proper particular scope. Kant knew, of course, that no single grammar could adequately represent every mode of human discourse, and that, though they bore certain inner resemblances to each other, no one of these could be substituted for any one or all of the others. In circumscribing the range of "pure reason," Kant recog-

30. In referring to "the reflexive turn," we are borrowing language employed by Pierre Thevenaz in *What Is Phenomenology?* (Chicago: Quadrangle Books, 1962).

nized that certain key items of religious belief could not be confirmed by the grammatical apparatus which could be applied to objects for which sense-data was also available. On the other hand, he acknowledged that some of these items had a formal capacity and function in that standard grammatical apparatus, but the apparatus itself was not able to substantiate the existence of any of these terms beyond the necessity of their formal functioning. To confirm their existence, Kant believed that one must move to another grammar in which their formal capacity was also matched by real content. And, thus, in speaking about most of the crucial items in religious belief, Kant shifted from a description of pure intellection to a methodical representation of moral sensitivity. Both of these efforts, one must add, were effected by means of the so-called reflexive turn.

Seen in this light, the response to Kant offered by Johannes Metz seems to consist almost entirely of an attempt to duplicate Kant's reflexive turn. Instead of trying to add content to Kant's results, that is, rather than tinkering with the grammar in a material way, Metz seems to be willing to repeat and further extend the methodological innovation which is responsible for them. Metz seems to be saying that it is enough to apply the reflexive turn to still another range of human experience, namely, the world of man's socio-political interdependencies. This is modal extension or methodological repetition, but it registers almost exclusively in formal terms. Metz seems to think that whatever content is necessary will follow from an extension of the reflexive turn. In short, as he sees it, the Christian horizon is recast through the shift to socio-criticism. What he fails to see, and this is a damaging criticism, is that grammars do not create or construct anything which was not there prior to the taking of the reflexive turn. A grammar is useful in bringing forms of symbolization to self-consciousness. They do this by exercising a certain second-order function. But they cannot be relied upon to produce first-order realities. A grammar can isolate the rules of the game, but a grammar is not that game itself.

And it is a colossal mistake, or, in the polite phrase, a category-error, to think that a grammar and a horizon are one and the same. Not even formally do they serve the same function. Kant provided a grammar, but only by a series of intricate steps can a grammar ever become a horizon. For horizons are first- rather than second-order phenomena. They are constitutive of experience and not representations of it. They give form to human aspirations, and do not simply record them. They attribute agency to religious belief and not just acceptable composure. To think that the mere duplication of Kant's reflexive turn (as noble and as difficult as that might be) can bring Christian belief through the Enlightenment to the present is to misconstrue the primary thrust of critical philosophy. Horizons do not issue from an exercising of critical reflexivity, even when the point of application is the socio-political world.

Nevertheless, given the above provisos, what Metz seems to be suggesting is that the turn to the world of human history gives one better access to the God Christians worship than is possible in any other perspective. In this respect, human history and socio-political involvement become more effective religious mooring points than human subjectivity. Their effectiveness derives in large part from the way in which they place religious persons under obligation to employ normative Christian action toward the realization of the content of freedom, peace, and justice. This is the hoped-for result of Johannes Metz's proposals. As such, it is also a central feature of the school of hope, a school in which he serves as a prime practitioner.

FIVE

On
Mapping a Hope
School

For the followers of these movements the creative future is
more important than the nostalgic past, because such movements are in reality new syntheses and in any case in dis-
agreement with the actual tradition. Thus the religion of
return appears in history as a creative religion of renewal.
—Vittorio Lanternari

The foregoing discussion of the standpoints from which
Ernst Bloch, Jürgen Moltmann, and Johannes Metz approach
their respective contentions regarding hope should illustrate
that the three men work from widely varying backgrounds
and on strikingly divergent sets of interests. The diversity
between them is so great that it is something of a marvel
that the three of them ever became associated in anything
like a common school. Certainly there are affinities between
them, but many of these are more occasional than deep-
seated. And the points at which they do converge are often
neither central nor fundamental to the positions of any of
them.

One can reinforce this observation by referring to the
characteristics of the hope school most often cited when
attempts are made to identify it. It is often said, for example, and with good reason, that the orientation of the hope
school is apocalyptic. Indeed, it is claimed further that the
school's apocalyptic temper is its chief identifying feature;

thus, much of the intrigue it creates derives from the hints it gives of reviving apocalypticism as the principal motif of earliest Christianity. And, as is well known, the support for that revival comes in large part from two respected biblical scholars—Gerhard von Rad and Ernst Käsemann—who have argued very impressively that the same motif, particularly in the New Testament, is the sine qua non of biblical understanding. Consequently, in drawing upon the results of such biblical scholarship, the proponents of the hope position can claim that their proposals enjoy both relevancy and scriptural authority.

Certainly Jürgen Moltmann argues that way, and, with much stretching and pulling, Ernst Bloch can also be interpreted as a supporter of the contention. But when one turns from Moltmann (and Bloch) to Metz, he finds no conscious attempt whatsoever to revive apocalyptic tendencies in the New Testament or even to lean upon their presence. Metz is simply not an apocalyptic thinker.[1] For him, the interest in a theology of hope does not occur under the banner of a revived apocalypticism, but, instead, as an expression of a newly found and negotiable involvement in the world. To say that Metz is not an apocalyptic thinker is not to say that he is not an eschatological thinker. Clearly he is the latter; and this, of course, is made evident in the attention he gives to developing a "creative militant eschatology" as well as in such statements as "God is the pressure for maturity exercised upon men who recognize that heaven and hell are real possibilities." But the imagery he selects does not bespeak the cataclysmic frenzy of worlds in conflict, the radical opposition between forces of light and the armies

1. One of the large differences between Moltmann and Metz, then, is that the former takes his orientation from Bloch's *Geist der Utopie* and the latter takes his from Rahner's *Geist in Welt,* and the subjects of "utopie" and "welt" are not the same.

of darkness, and its accompanying anti-establishment tendencies. Neither has Metz seen fit to make definite distinction between a chosen group of people—Moltmann's apocalyptic community or Bloch's commonwealth of freedom—and the others, even within Christendom, whose social position is not so radicalized. Rather, Metz's interest in "the last things" is a major focus of his concern for the care of the world. Rather than being a theological articulation of apocalyptic motifs, his thought is rightly termed "a theology of the world."

Similarly, as noted before, Metz's entrance into that "world" derives not so much from preoccupation with trends in social history as it does from long-standing epistemological dilemmas. His interest in secularism, for example, should not be construed as an interest in placing the present moment in a much larger chronological series. He does not look at secularism with a view toward cultivating a more acute sensitivity to "the specific tendency of things in this latter age," but, instead, as a theological test case. His claim is that secularism must be accepted—that is, the secularity of the world must be taken as an evident fact—by any Christian who understands himself to be taking the world seriously. As Metz views it, secularism is the context to which all theological statements must eventually make reference. It is the setting in which they are concretized. Thus, to accept secularism as a given in theological reflection is to make sure that such reflection can be called a theology of the world.

One suspects that the same is also true of Metz's interest in Marxism. From outward appearances, it looks as if Metz does not regard Karl Marx as a theorist in whose thought one finds oneself naturally immersed, or as one one necessarily encounters in the path that impels one toward the truth. One can be certain that Metz did not come upon Marx as one reaching out for something reliable on which to get a firm foothold, but, instead, that he encountered Marx when he cultivated familiarization with the world. It simply happens that Karl Marx is the most influential ideologist for a great many living European people, and this fact must be acknowledged too in one's acceptance of the secularity of the world. Indeed, much of the impetus for secularity stems from the writings of Karl Marx. Thus, interest in Marx need be neither personal nor passionate, but rather more like the doctoral candidate's recognition that his field of competency cannot be mastered until he has come to terms with the most influential figures within it.

And the same is true also with respect to Metz's attitude to Ernst Bloch. Bloch does not stand as Metz's teacher, or even as his guide or liberator. Instead, Metz recognizes that he is living, at least to some extent, in a world made articulate by the writings of Ernst Bloch. Hence, as spokesman to and for the world, the author of *Das Prinzip Hoffnung* and *Atheismus im Christentum* becomes one from whom Metz receives insights and also one with whom he quarrels. As a theologian, Johannes Metz does not stand to the philosopher Ernst Bloch in the same way, for example (to choose a classic case), that St. Thomas Aquinas stood to Aristotle. Bloch does not provide the reliable conceptual framework within which authoritative religious truth can be expressed; nor, for Metz, is he the best representative of the philosophical stance which is most compelling. Metz is really not "Blochian" in the way Jürgen Moltmann might be, nor is Moltmann "Blochian" in the way Thomas Aquinas might be called "Aristotelian." For that matter, Moltmann has probably been influenced more by Karl Barth than by Ernst Bloch—since he uses Barth in criticism of Bloch—and Johannes Metz's principal theological and philosophical mentors are Karl Rahner and Martin Heidegger. But, with his background, Moltmann would have found it natural to spend long hours in Marxist theory, for the problematic with which Moltmann and Marxist theoreticians begin, namely, alienation, is couched in strikingly similar terms. For Moltmann, Marxist theory provides one viable response to fundamental human (particularly socio-political) problems. For Metz, on the other hand, Marxism is encountered primarily in the Christian's brush with the world.

It has also become somewhat fashionable to link the three chief spokesmen for the hope school on the basis of their adherence to "process thought." They have been referred to, even here, as "process thinkers." But, unless carefully distinguished, this too can be misleading, and not simply by reason of the fact that Henri Bergson, Alfred North Whitehead, Charles Hartshorne (and the other recognized representatives of that stance) play no conscious formative role in the development of their contentions. Only one of the three figures—Ernst Bloch—can ever be classified as a "process thinker"; and this is permissible in Bloch's case only if one adds quickly that Bloch is certainly also manifestly atypical. It would be fair to say that Bloch's thought exhibits certain tendencies which are characteristic of process thought and which agree with other process patterns. However, if one were to use those patterns as clues to the theologies of both Moltmann and Metz, he would find them shockingly out of bounds. Metz is not a process thinker, except at times only grudgingly, and whatever "process" tendencies Moltmann reflects can be much better accounted for by reference to other criteria. Both resemble process thinkers because the end modular result of their theological innovations is a horizontal depiction of Christian affirmations. Their thought is "process" rather than "essentialist" because of its tendency toward horizontal rather than vertical projection. And that formal tendency leads to other formal characteristics which a number of other so-called process thinkers share. But in no sense is it true that process philosophy stands as a schematic a priori to hope theology. Chronologically, this is certainly not true; that is, Moltmann and Metz did not become acquainted with the conceptual possibilities inherent in process thought, recognizing the advantages they might offer the theologian, then set out to provide a new articulation of the Christian faith in such terms. It did not happen that way. As a matter of fact, neither of the two theologians is very conversant with very much of process thought. Similarly, it is not true either that process thought stands as a logical or formal condition of hope theology. What the theologians say can be said without reference to process categories and process terminology. However, since both process thought and hope theology build upon horizontal schematizing, they do resemble each other in many formal respects. For example, both give much attention to the future time. Both prefer dynamic over static categories. Both give primacy to such modes of awareness as intuition and insight. Both expend every effort to keep life moving freely. Both give great place to the kind of personal industry that goes by the name of creativity. And both place a premium on the creative influence of human decision-making. When this latter stress is converted into a slogan, it declares that man's decisions have a definite influence upon the eventual shape of the world.

In summary, the school of hope resembles process thought in a large variety of ways, but without being a direct implicate or a derivative. In the articulation of its own proposals, it finds itself employing a horizontal model and the language of process philosophy from time to time. But the model and the terminology belong no more exclusively to the one orientation than they do to the other. And the occurrence of process talk in the theology of hope camp should not be taken as an indication that the two have formed an alliance. At the same time, there are no reasons why the two cannot stand together as mutual aids. It is obvious that the theology of hope would be more substantial if, in crucial areas, it had benefited from the experience of process thinkers, who, at least conceptually and formally, have met similar intellectual dilemmas before.

We have noted that all linear conceptual patterns, when their theological overtones are gathered up, turn out to be tacitly atheistic. This is a bold statement in theological circles, and it needs to be qualified. It simply means that the horizontal model gives place to God either as an eventual possibility (toward which the process is moving), or, less often, as the reconciling agent who works possibilities into the formative stream of things. When God is assigned the first of these roles, it is appropriate to say—as Jürgen Moltmann does—that "there is no God yet." Or, in proper Blochian language, Moltmann can say that God belongs to the range of things "still not yet." Johannes Metz, following the same tendency, refers to the knowledge of God that accrues to responsible, purposeful moral action, and, in so doing, seems to have come close to the view that from no other stance is God humanly accessible. And, of course, the chief proponent of this tendency within the hope school is Ernst Bloch himself, particularly in his book *Atheismus im Christentum,* in which he contends that "only an atheist can be a good Christian, [and] only a Christian can be a good atheist." His contention is based on the argument that the full development of human potentialities requires the transformation of the universe into a home for man. Jesus, the revolutionary religious leader, inspired men to create a rich, full, and beautiful utopian future. Thus, the motivation which comes from early Christianity stands in radical contrast to the destructive despair of nihilism, on the one hand, and the typical tendency of many well-meaning people to squander their goods on some imaginary transcendent being called "God."[2] Nihilism is shallow and trivial, according to Bloch, and belief in God leads to an impoverishment of human life. But the spirit which stems from Jesus, which is neither nihilistic nor theistic, in Bloch's view, leads to an advancement of a better world. (Once again, the pattern is the same: the theistic God, the conserver of permanence, stands opposed to humanistic dynamic questing for a future upon which man is dependent for the realization of his potentialities.) Commenting on Bloch's contention, Jürgen Moltmann has written with approval as well as criticism:

"Only an atheist can be a good Christian," Bloch had written. In my contribution to the *Festschrift* I reversed this: "Only a Christian can be a good atheist." Bloch accepted the offer. But what is atheism? Is it the abandonment of a God different from man (as Feuerbach thought), so that God and man will come to be of one essence? In that case atheism would be the acme of mysticism. Or is it the perfect insight into the different being of God and man, in the expectation of future correspondence and communion?[3]

Then, after noting ways in which the kind of atheism Bloch espouses can be refined and developed into a negative theology, Moltmann writes that

Christian theology may join hands with the "atheistic" principle of hope: first, in fighting all those who would break man of the habit of questioning and casting doubt on his unhappy circumstances, so as to make him a well-adjusted functionary or consumer; and secondly, in finding the "traces" of man's

2. Cf. Bloch's essay, "Christian Social Utopias," in *Man On His Own*, trans. E. B. Ashton (New York: Herder and Herder, 1970), pp. 118–41.

3. Jürgen Moltmann, "Introduction," in *Man On His Own*, p. 28.

coming homeland and helping him fight for freedom and justice in a society that would entwine him with itself.[4]

The principle built into the horizontal scheme, namely, the perpetual refusal to acknowledge that the status quo is all there is, is given large expression in the hope orientations. Indeed, this is a cardinal feature of any thought pattern which is motivated by linear projection, and works to guide present tendencies to a future culmination. The presence of that principle in hope thought has particular influence upon the way in which the church as an institution is understood. Every member of the hope school is critical of the church, and, for all of them, criticism comes to focus on the church's built-in resistance to change and its suspicions regarding revolution and innovation. Ernst Bloch believes, for example, that the courageous message of the revolutionary figure, Jesus of Nazareth, stands diametrically opposed to the subsequent interpretation of his message by Jesus' followers, particularly St. Paul. According to Bloch, Jesus was a social revolutionary, a utopian visionary, who believed "economic questions" were "senseless," who "regarded the 'present aeon' as finished . . . and believed in the immediately impending cosmic disaster."[5] As depicted in the Bible, in Bloch's view, Christianity is utopian in an almost unqualified sense. Being utopian, it was not "otherworldly," however, for the kingdom of God which Jesus proclaimed did not refer to something beyond this world which was geographically transcendent, but, instead, to a "succession in time on the same stage, here on earth."

> The goal was not a beyond after death, where the angels sing; it was the terrestrial as well as supraterrestrial kingdom of love, with its first enclave already constituted by the original community. Not until after the catastrophe of the cross was

4. Ibid., p. 29.
5. Bloch, "Christian Social Utopias," p. 124.

the kingdom of the other world interpreted as lying in the beyond. Above all, it would be so interpreted once the Pilates (and especially the Neros) had become Christian themselves; what was all-important to the ruling class was that the love-communism be relaxed as spiritually as possible. To Jesus, the kingdom of this world was that of the devil (John 8, 44). This is why he never suggested allowing it to go on; he did not conclude a non-aggression pact with it. He rejected armed force. . . . Arms are rejected because to the apocalypt Jesus they are already obsolete, hence superfluous. He expects an upheaval that will leave no stone unturned anyway, and he expects it at any moment, from nature, from the superweapon of a cosmic catastrophe.[6]

In subsequent preaching and teaching, the sharpness of Jesus' message was severely diminished, its outcry against the status quo was tempered, and the result was Pauline Christianity:

What men longed for was something totally different, some-thing totally new, and the eventual victor in the competition of salvations—victorious by making political use of the new— was Pauline Christianity.[7]

And the result was also the identification of the kingdom of God with the church. Bloch describes the transition: "Instead of a radical renewal of this world, an institute of the beyond appeared—the church—and interpreted the Christian social utopia as referring to itself."[8] The church, in short, stands in direct contrast to Jesus' ultimate intention. It is the product of a combination of loss of nerve, on the one hand, and mistaken identity on the other. In the passage of time, the Christians sought future consolation more reso-lutely than a fresh start on a new earth.

Moltmann's and Metz's attitudes to the church are similar in tone to Bloch's. When they are negative, both tend to see the church in institutional terms, and consider much of

6. Ibid., p. 123.
7. Ibid., p. 125.
8. Ibid., p. 126.

what it stands for to be a surrogate for the real. For both, Jesus' revolutionary message must often be placed in contrast to many of the preoccupations of official Christianity. Though, on this score, Moltmann is exceedingly more "Protestant" than Metz.

As a Protestant, and as a champion of an apocalyptic stance, it is appropriate for Moltmann to be critical of any organism which likes to foster "an institutional stabilizing of things." In the book *Theology of Hope,* in the chapter on the "Exodus Church"—and the imagery is fitting—Moltmann writes about the conflict which is imposed on every Christian:

> If the God who called them to life should expect of them something more than what modern industrial society expects and requires of them, then Christians must venture an exodus and regard their social roles as a new Babylonian exile. Only where they appear in society as a group which is not wholly adaptable and in the case of which the modern integration of everything (when) with everything else fails to succeed, do they enter into a conflict-laden, but fruitful partnership with this society. Only where their resistance shows them to be a group that is incapable of being assimilated or of "making the grade," can they communicate their own hope to this society. They will then be led in this society to a constant unrest which nothing can allay or bring to accommodation and rest.[9]

In that setting, the function of whatever church there is is to offer the kind of resistance to the status quo which makes things uncertain, and thus, by contrast, to cultivate the occasion to point to the expected kingdom of God. In a dramatic statement of this task, Moltmann contends that Christian hope itself will endeavor

> to lead our modern institutions away from their own immanent tendency towards stabilization, will make them uncertain, historify them and open them to that elasticity which is demanded by openness towards the future for which it hopes.[10]

9. Jürgen Moltmann, *Theology of Hope,* trans. James W. Leitch (London: SCM Press, and New York: Harper and Row, 1967), p. 324.
10. Ibid., p. 330.

While the author of *Theology of Hope* would not fall prey to any demand that he distinguish the true Christian church from all false Christian churches, it is obvious that he looks to certain eschatologically oriented task forces (creative disciples who effect their own exodus from the world by reference to a horizon of future expectation) as exemplifying the identifying characteristics of the Christian church.

For Johannes Metz, a priest in the Catholic Church, it is not that easy. Metz would very much like to develop his political theology, even his creative militant eschatology, without standing in judgment over the fundamental institutional tendencies of Roman Catholicism. Hence, on the one side, he subscribes to the belief that there is salvation in the church, and, from the other side, he is critical of any simple identification of the church with the kingdom of God. He does not want to idolize or eternalize the church, and yet he believes it performs a valuable function even in more radically eschatological terms. Metz seeks reform of the church, but the kind of reform which is more renovation than death and new birth. His argument is that the established church can become an effective political instrument to criticize the status quo because its existence points to a reality beyond itself. Because it is oriented to the future, it need not expend its most precious energies in maintaining its position and status in contemporary society.

> As institution the church itself lives under the eschatological proviso. It is not for itself; it does not serve its own self-affirmation, but the historical affirmation of the salvation of all men. The hope it announces is hope, not for the church, but for the kingdom of God. As institution, the church truly lives on the proclamation of its own eschatological stipulation in that it establishes itself as the institution of critical liberty, in the fact of society and its absolute and self-sufficient claims.[11]

11. Johannes B. Metz, "Religion and Society in Light of a Political Society," in *The Future of Hope,* ed. Walter H. Capps (Philadephia: Fortress Press, 1970), p. 146.

Metz recognizes, however, that the church will become an effectively critical socio-political force only if it accepts a new understanding of itself. He acknowledges that the church is not yet a "second-order institution," namely, one which lives to foster critical consciousness; but he believes that signs are present which point to this transformation. If the transformation could occur, the church would see itself not as the author of a system of social doctrine but as the practitioner of social criticism. The underlying thesis is apparent: the church understands "the whole of history to stand under God's eschatological proviso."

Metz differs with Moltmann on two large points. First, he sees no intrinsic gap between "official" and "true" Christianity. That is, he does not mistrust the institutional form of Christianity in all of the ways Moltmann is disposed to. Nor is there suggestion in Metz that a small group of people, from the beginning of Christian history, have exhibited a special sensitivity to Jesus' message, which, by contrast, has gone largely misconstrued in traditional and institutional circles. In Metz's writings, there is no attempt to write any "tale of two cities" within Christian history. He makes no distinction, for example, between people with eschatological vision and the others. Nor does he assert that finally, at long last, an interpretation of the faith has been cultivated which is in keeping with the New Testament outlook, as opposed to those many other kinds of interpretation which are manifestly misleading. Both Moltmann and Bloch charge an early misinterpretation of the gospel responsible for the departure of many from the radically eschatological, that is, apocalyptic vision. Both of them also explain the founding of official, institutional Christianity in those terms. Both use the contrast to recommend a form of "authentic" Christianity which in Bloch's terms is revolutionarily utopian and in Moltmann's terms is oriented toward a future hope. Metz has no preferred alternative to institutional Christianity, but he does want to build some of the characteristics of Moltmann's and Bloch's version into the church's current posture. Yet, though the three men differ on specific points in this regard, they are together in trying to qualify institutional life by the realities referred to most aptly in horizontal terminology. All three would agree that vital, vibrant, enervating, and resourceful Christianity is the kind which understands that the world is not yet finished, and that the new cannot simply be peeled off of the things which already are.

Their attitudes to the present world differ markedly also. Neither Bloch nor Moltmann feels quite at home in the present scheme of things; indeed, the very occasion for their proposals is the discrepancy between what is and what yearns to be. Moltmann argues repeatedly that Christian hope calls into question the things which already are by virtue of its commitment to a promised future. And Bloch refers just as often to the unconditionality of man's utopian future which relativizes the present aeon and places it in series with the plans which are to be unveiled. Characteristically, both Bloch and Moltmann juxtapose man's present homelessness against the attainment of his homeland in the awaited future. Bloch speaks about the home of eventual identity; man will know who he is when he comes home. The imagery, once again, is that of the ship moving toward its destination, the harbor standing as the place of identity. Moltmann, too, reinforces Bloch's imagery in talking about "man's coming homeland," and the traces one can detect of it in present society.

Men who are questing after an envisioned homeland cannot possibly feel at home where they are. Consequently, the kind of religious affirmations which develop from the feeling of homelessness is that which befits the diaspora.

The writings of Moltmann and Bloch give articulation to many of the sensitivities which belong to a diaspora people: a people scattered outside their true homeland, and living presently in virtual exile. Of course, the same temperament also applies to apocalyptic communities, as Bloch and Moltmann both recognize and document. Apocalypticism is a diaspora phenomenon. Its very mood depends upon an awareness of being scattered away from a normative place and existing in anticipation of a normative time. Similarly, it is customary for diaspora peoples to understand themselves as being pilgrims or wayfarers in their present state. Because they are in exile, they have no interest in setting down deep roots; they are wary of all established institutions which do not recognize the fragility and temporary character of the present scheme of things. The hymns and prayers they develop express the sighs and longings of people who are waiting for their deliverance. And, in waiting for an eventual release from the bondage in which they must suffer, they are trained to watch for signs, to be expectant regarding events, and to be perceptive with respect to the shifts which are bound to occur in their present albeit temporary environment. Moltmann and Bloch capture the mood of that longing; they are sensitive to the cherished expectations of a diaspora people.

But in giving articulation to a corporate hope of long-centuries standing, whose adherents have been present in almost every locale, Bloch and Moltmann also reveal many of their own attitudes to the present world. By what they have disclosed, one can observe that neither man feels completely at home here. Neither can relax in the thought that the present world is good and meant to be enjoyed. Indeed, one can understand Moltmann's more recent turn to a theology of play, following the era of a theology of hope, as a necessary corrective to a previous overstress. It is a corrective, a mitigator, which is registered in keeping with one of Moltmann's crucial methodological principles, namely, that "a thing is alive only when it contains contradiction in itself" and has "the power of holding the contradiction within itself and enduring it." And yet the very language of the slogan in which the new stress is included, namely, "How can one play in a strange land?" confirms the suspicion that it belongs to an extended understanding of diaspora religion. The new theology of play simply indicates that one can find some enjoyment even in a world which is not yet home; but the play which transpires there is not free of ironic and often bizarre, carnivallike tendencies. Men's play in exile is not identical in either form or quality to the playing which is appropriate in the presence of God. Even when at play, man cannot rid himself of the consciousness that where he is is not the same as where he must eventually be. And the distances between the two can only be overcome by a voyage on man's part, and a reconciling series of events which originate in God.

Sensing that they are not yet at home, both Bloch and Moltmann live in a bifurcated world. For them, the world is not yet one. Thus, human experience is fragmented, piecemeal, and shot through with inequities, inconsistencies, and deceptions. It is not enough that one seek to find the *center* of human experience, the center of the world, or (though the language is not quite appropriate) the center of reality, and then work to become aware of its presence. If that were possible, proper orientation to the world would flow from a discovery of its *center,* followed by a deliberate and disciplined attempt to keep the center in proper focus. But, for Moltmann and Bloch, there is no center. The world has no visible or perceptible mooring point. One could find no normative place of orientation, except in the future, in a place which is not yet and can be realized through an exercising of a rite of passage. It is not the case that God is the center of human life, and that man falters because he does not recognize this. If that were the case, human salvation would accrue to intuitive insight. But that is not the case. Man's situation in the world is far more radical than that. It is also somewhat more complex. For instead of its being the case that God is *in* the center, or that God *is* the center, which man, to his peril, does not recognize, it is the case that God is not that center. Conceivably, God should be that center, but this has not been accomplished, at least not yet. And the world, as a result, has no center. Lacking a center, the world can nevertheless not get along without one. But that is precisely the problem. There is no center though a center really ought to be. Indeed, there can be no center in a bifurcated world. Instead, in lieu of a present center there is simply a reliable point of orientation in a future whose reality is present now only in hope and promise. The point of orientation will have become visible when the fundamental bifurcation is challenged and conquered. And that is the event for which the pilgrim people, the diaspora communities, sigh with expectant longing.

Johannes Metz, in distinction to Ernst Bloch and Jürgen Moltmann, does not live in a bifurcated world. For him, the world is already one, no matter how difficult it is to give that contention articulation. Hence, Metz does not find it necessary to jettison Christendom (as Bloch, Moltmann, Bonhoeffer, and even Harnack are sometimes prepared to do) in order to make space available for some truer norm. He recognizes that Christendom must be refurbished. It must be trained in new skills and equipped with new sets of navigational instruments. But it need not be voluntarily sacrificed because it threatens man's ultimate welfare. The church can become impoverished; it can find itself in a position in which it is no longer in tune with those who recognize that heaven and hell are also real secular possibilities; it can also fail to sense the manifold ramifications of a world which is pluralistic. But a pluralistic world is not simply bifurcated. And a recognition of the worldliness of the world, as Metz exhorts, is something of which the present church is at least tacitly capable. Such a recognition does not pose any unqualified threat to the church. Nor need it be destructive of Christendom. In short, because he lives in a world in which harmony and unifying order are both implicit, no matter how fragile, Johannes Metz can accept Dietrich Bonhoeffer's transition from theory to action without coupling it with an attack on Christendom. For Metz, a "world come of age" would not be a world in which anti-institutionalism is maximized in favor of an apocalyptic alternative. Instead, the "world come of age" is a world in which the hominization of every sphere of human life has been set in motion. Metz firmly believes that the faith of the fathers—and not simply the faith of the anti-fathers— can become resourceful in a world oriented to the future.

For Moltmann and Bloch, such resourcefulness comes to require an interpretation of that faith which is carefully distinguished. For Bloch, the normative reading of the Bible is that which takes place in the underground. The Bible is read differently there, he notices; and Moltmann agrees that "Bloch's reading of the Bible is not the one we are used to." People who are at home in the world normally do not dwell in the underground. Some who do live there, however, like the most perceptive of Plato's cave dwellers, come to sense that "reality" is both outside and future. They also come to interpret their lives as being bondage-ridden, and salvation in terms of the liberty they wait to enjoy. In that setting, it is appropriate to magnify the distinction between darkness and light with reference to the contrast between the present state and hoped-for salvation. It is also fitting that dwellers in the underground recognize that their present habitat cannot be used as an accurate index into the general character of things. To do that would be to take a partial glimpse for a total picture, and to lose whatever magnificence there is through a fundamental impoverishment. It is also entirely characteristic of their estate for dwellers in underground places of refuge to regard the rest of mankind as enemies and perpetual threats. In so doing, those who understand themselves as diaspora peoples also know that the regimes which keep them in exile must be overthrown by dramatic (if not always violent) means. In that setting, the Bible is read differently than it is by those who do not sense that the world is split and who are not conscious of any real exile. For diaspora people, religion is not just something one thinks about.

But Bloch's observation goes much deeper. If, as Ernst Käsemann contends, "apocalypticism is the mother of all theology," then the Bible is really an underground book. It stems from and belongs to the underground. It vents the aspirations of a diaspora people. And, if that be the case, it is a manual which guides men who are so inspired to conduct a revolution. Outside the underground, where the bifurcation is either unrecognized or denied, the Bible serves as a kind of apologia for the things which already are. And this is precisely Feuerbach's, Marx's, Bloch's, and Moltmann's point. Status quo religion affirms the God of permanence and works to keep oppressed people in clandestine conspiratorial cells. The dynamic, future-directed utopian-oriented religious alternative does not belong to establishment peoples. And the contrast between the two makes it imperative that our next chapter should seriously consider the possibility that the Christian religion has in fact developed along two opposing lines. Is it possible that there are, and have been, two religions of Christianity?

SIX

The Two
Religions of
Christianity

. . . two irreconcilable opinions had fluctuated hither and
thither, and had been accepted and acknowledged by men,
according as they were of a more active or passive nature.

—Goethe

The advent of a theology of hope during the past few years
has raised a number of questions about the morphology of
religious consciousness in the Western world. Are Christians
able to accept the "God ahead"—the *Gott vor uns* of
Johannes Metz[1]—or are they restricted by tradition and
temperament to a "God above"? Can they regard the future
as the locus of their religious norm, or are they compelled
by training and habit to fix that norm in the past? Do they
possess sufficient resourcefulness or flexibility to give credence to theological positions which are horizontally
ordered, or must they insist upon vertical projection? Is
there a place in their attitudes for "process," or are they
unconditionally committed to "substance"? Can their interests and affirmations be correlated with "actional categories,"
or does supplementation of the theoretical attitude lead to

1. Metz's most dramatic statements in this regard occur in his essay,
"Gott vor uns," in *Ernst Bloch zu Ehren*, ed, Siegfried Unseld (Frankfurt: Suhrkamp Verlag, 1965), pp. 227–41.

a loss of all order? To raise questions of this kind is not only to record some of the issues nascent in the proposals of Ernst Bloch, Jürgen Moltmann, and Johannes Metz; it is also to argue that those same proposals belong to a dialectic. One can observe this simply from the proposals' form. They are always presented in a juxtapositional manner. They always proceed by drawing contrasts. They seek support by playing upon antinomies. To be sure, the proposals themselves are both striking and novel, for they set themselves in contraposition to points of view which own greater longevity, tacit institutional sanction, as well as the tested ability to support both personal and church piety. In short, the contrasts out of which Moltmann's and Metz's recommendations are drawn seem to require, as their designers admit, a reshaping of traditional Christian religious sensitivities. In every case, and on every issue, the position of the "hope school" runs contrary to an antinomical correspondent.

There are a number of ways of accounting for the apparent success of this attempt to shift polar axes. One can argue that the recent interest in concepts of hope is the theological counterpart to the rather widespread concern about the future in contemporary culture. One can support this claim by pointing to the increasing amount of preoccupation with "the future of mankind" on the part of industrial managers, design scientists, ethicists, statesmen, and men from a host of other fields and disciplines. It is obvious that the future has taken on a special prominence in the present moment. Each day one can find additional evidence of the intrigue and the challenges it creates. Hence, one can justify the shift—or rupture—in religious consciousness which hope theology seems to imply by referring to the more widespread transition which the future-orientation effects everywhere. Everything which becomes part of the preoccupation with "the future of mankind" is forbidden to remain simply as it was apart from that alliance. The shape of theological positions is no different. When theology's affirmations are referred to the concerns about the future, they assume a different shape than that by which they were previously characterized. The context of the future-orientation carries the formal ability to influence the content of anything that seeks inclusion in it. Hence, the shift implicit in theology is a kind of refraction of the larger shift which occurred when men's interests were governed by the future.

But there is another way of approaching the novel appearance of hope theology which is more to its proponents' likings. That way is to refer its radical character to the radical character of early Christian teaching. On this basis one can argue that the new theology is in fact a repristination of an earlier perspective: a perspective which represents the mind of the earliest Christian community. From this standpoint, hope theology would not be new. Its radicality is no more severe than the radicality of the first century Christian outlook. By implication, the change of perspective called for in the present time is an attempt to recapture the nucleus of the "normative faith." That normative stance, so the interpretation goes, had become lost in the succession of formalisms which superseded the simplicity of the first century vision. The mistake that needs to be righted is the rupture which found original "hope theology" supplanted. In proper language, the product of the hellenization of the kerygma, formal Christianity, was not only a radical break with the past, but also represents a mistaken turn.

Because they take recourse to this second way of placing the shift, the theologians of hope are sympathetic to the historical chronicle which writers like Leslie Dewart have made familiar. In his provocative book *The Future of Belief:*

Theism in a World Come of Age,[2] Dewart argues that the culprit in the desolution of Christian truth from the beginning until now is the hellenized intruder who, once he is admitted on his own terms, proceeds to order all of Christian affirmation by means of his own thought categories. The product of hellenization is a beauty to behold. It is systematically coherent, neatly unified, self-referential, and aesthetically pleasing. But, it has not retained the sense of the earliest gospel. The first century norm can be recaptured only if the hellenized format which has been given to it is stripped away. Hence, Dewart calls for a radical—note the recurrence of "radical"—"dehellenization" of the kerygma. The purpose is to remove the alien elements, and to restore the initial presentation to a position of singular power.

In principle, but not in substance, Dewart's proposals are not very much different from those voiced at the turn of the century by the famous historian of dogma, Adolf von Harnack, of the University of Berlin. Nor are they completely unlike the interests often ascribed (especially by Harnack) to Martin Luther. In all three cases, there was an attempt to restore the primitive kerygma by preserving it from its subsequent associations with patterns of systematic thought whose origins lay in Greek philosophy. In each interpretation, the imposition of Greek thought and language forms upon an original core-element was understood to imply a transition in consciousness whose effect was not altogether salutary.

The theologians of hope would be sympathetic to the same line of reasoning. They too are obliged to demonstrate that the positions they seek to supplant are erroneously

2. Leslie Dewart, *The Future of Belief: Theism in a World Come of Age* (New York: Herder and Herder, 1966).

based, and are not necessary to Christianity's fundamental disposition. The extent to which they are able to make their case is the extent to which they can mitigate the so-called radical character of their suggestions. They admit that what they are proposing requires a radical shift if it is to be understood or implemented. But that shift is restorative in nature. The theology of hope is radical, but no more radical—so say its adherents—than the affirmations of earliest Christianity.

The general questions which emerge from this kind of discussion concern the formal dynamics of theological reflection. The changes which hope theology implies are changes of conceptual structure and not simply changes of content. Or, to put the matter more exactly, changes in theological content accompany changes in conceptual structure. And to suggest that hope theology is a dialectical position is to argue that Christian religious consciousness is two-sided. It sees things in at least two different ways. The theology of hope gives expression to one of these two sides; the positions against which it is juxtaposed express the corresponding other side. In hope theology the two sides have been made antagonistic to each other. But in religious consciousness the two sides must learn to live with each other. But we must be more specific.

I would like to argue that the Christian religion has been formed by two contrary dispositions. By the one, men have been inspired toward things not of this world; by the other, men have been encouraged to foster care of this world. Both of these fundamental tendencies have been implicit in Christian attitudes and expressions—in theology, liturgy, art, architecture, and social and political sensitivity—since the New Testament era. Each has its own myths and stories. Each, on its own, could support a ritualistic system. Though the stresses would vary, each, on its own, could provide a program of social action. The verbal side of each of the two strains can be translated into a consistent doctrinal scheme. Neither disposition, furthermore, is an outgrowth of the other. Neither can be reduced to the other. Both resist conjunction or partnership in some larger, higher, or more comprehensive unity. Each refuses to be subordinated to the other. Neither is a mode or an aspect of something else. Indeed, each carries the requisite formal apparatus as well as sufficient materials to be able to inspire and inhabit a fully expressible religious consciousness. Yet, the two formative dispositions have cohabited under the auspices of a single formal religion.

By the one disposition has come the inspiration for seeking that for which human experience provides no common analogues. From the other issues a motivation for hallowing human experience for what it is in itself. "Religion A" has cultivated sensitivity to the sort of transcendence which is defined in contrast to all things natural. "Religion B" is trained to look for whatever transcendence there is in things as they are. Individual or personal salvation, in the first, derives from the awareness that beyond common human experience—or beneath, behind, or above it—rests a permanence whose reality is threatened only by man's failure to recognize it. In the second, human salvation depends upon corporate resourcefulness in facing and overcoming both the threat and the reality of nonpermanence. Hence, the disposition which moves toward a transcendent "otherness" also exhibits particular interest in the well-being of the individual; frequently it attempts to characterize the integrated, healthy, or whole personality by means of religious and devotional terminology. The second disposition, more often than not, seems almost willing to forego the priorities placed upon individual salvation, or to subsume them within a sensibility which assumes socio-political upheaval, intellectual unrest, and cultural transformation to be persistent religious necessities. Furthermore, in their map work, Religion A schematizes vertically and Religion B horizontally. The first disposition measures moral and ethical obligation by distinguishing "the higher" and "the lower." The second disposition makes use of the categories of time, and gains its impetus from the separation between present accomplishment and necessary ultimate realization.

Both fundamental dispositions can inspire and encourage an ethic and a theology. Each bespeaks integrated symbolic worlds. Each can be drawn upon to inspire and give direction to ritual and social action. Each would be able to foster its own set of creeds. And both have been existing together, matching each other in parallel fashion since the inception of the phenomenon called *Urchristentum.* Together they are responsible for much of the complexity, and, shall we also say the genius, of the Christian religion. Since the beginning that religion has been dual and not simply singular. It has thrived on that dialectical tension. From the beginning, there have been two religions of Christianity.

The hope thinkers themselves, furthermore, are not unaware of the differences between Religions A and B. Moltmann knows, for example, that Christianity is characterized by two distinctive tendencies, and Bloch calls attention to the fact that the Bible is read differently in establishment circles and in the underground. The hope theologians are eager to identify their own contentions with the first vision of Christians, a vision which stands in opposition to most of that which goes under the banner of "Christianity." Moltmann is specific on this point. He contends that the earliest Christian vision—in the normative Christian era—was weakened, then finally all but destroyed by the same kind of élan which produced Christendom.

And Christendom, in this context, means the product of the thoroughgoing formalization of the primitive religion. Moltmann's position is not unlike that of other Harnackian-influenced thinkers, Martin Werner in particular, who focus on the differences between the Christian outlook which obtained prior to the third and fourth centuries A.D. and the one which was manifest after the formalizing process had taken effect.[3] According to Werner, the religious outlook of Christians prior to the great era of formalization was characterized by its expectation of the kingdom of God. Early Christians lived within the consciousness that the kingdom of God was very near—near in both spatial and temporal terms. But this eschatological awareness was broken, first through disappointment, but subsequently through preoccupations of another kind. Instead of disposing themselves toward the immanence of the eschaton, an eschaton whose freshness had been dissipated by years of waiting, the Christians of subsequent centuries became more concerned about perpetuating an institution threatened from within by loss of confidence and without by rival philosophical parties. On the basis of this analysis, it is easy to regard "Christendom" as being some sort of deviant religious construct, since its existence implies the loss of an earlier authenticity, vitality, and freshness.

It is also appropriate, given this analysis, to regard the activities of the entire Middle Ages as being under Christendom's clouds. Similarly, this sort of analysis gives the Protestant historian ample basis on which to argue for the necessity of the Reformation. The Reformation looms up, then, as the era in which the tendencies leading to Christendom were reversed and the hellenization process was

3. Martin Werner, *The Formation of Christian Doctrine* (Boston: Beacon Press, 1965).

redressed. Luther, as has been mentioned, becomes the great restorer: the first one to ably and effectively rediscover and reestablish the pulse beat of the initial Christian vision. And, to bring the thrust of the analogy up-to-date, Moltmann's rediscovery of the initial pulse beat of the New Testament community can be likened to a Reformation event. It is reformatory in the sense that it recaptures that which was essential to the Christian vision prior to the time of its spoilation by the formalizing tendencies of Christendom. When Adolf von Harnack tells the story, the normative Christian vision is submerged from the mid-third until the sixteenth century. When Jürgen Moltmann tells the story the normative element is "underground" from some time following the church's judgment against Marcion until, it appears, just recently. But the story is fundamentally the same: First century Christian faith was born on the wings of a joyful expectation of the end times. When that vision weakened—both through inner disappointment and external obstacles—it was compensated for by a vertically oriented salvation scheme whose principal effect was to establish the necessity of a fortresslike religious institution. The vision responsible for first century Christian faith has not totally disappeared in the intervening years, however, but it certainly has not been prominent. Moltmann, like Harnack before him, finds it necessary to point out the differences between the normative vision and the orientation by which the normative vision has been supplanted. In both cases, there is an attempt to demonstrate that the present orientation is fundamentally out of line with the initial vision. But, in both cases, there is confidence that that initial vision can be reeffected. Indeed, in both cases, there is conviction that the initial vision is being reeffected, and that its rediscovery is necessary to the very survival of Christian inclinations.

Moltmann and Harnack before him sense the radical differences between two religions, both of which have enjoyed the name "Christian," although the first is less public than the second, and, as a result, both truer and more difficult to detect.

What this appraisal tends to overlook, however, is that vertically ordered Religion A is a concomitant of horizontally ordered Religion B. Religion B is born on the wings of Religion A, and, at the same time, is often the creator and sustainer of Religion A. The two religions require each other. They are not exclusive options. To cite but one instance of their complex interdependence, I should like to consider the way in which the theme of "kingship" registers within both of them.[4]

One of the distinguishing tendencies of the religion which uses vertical orientation is the way in which vertical hierarchization is employed as the basis of formalization. The hellenization of the kerygma, in Harnack's words, could have been accomplished by no other kind of formal schematization. And one of the surest signs of the presence of vertical hierarchization is the primacy accorded to the highest, which, by attribution belongs to the ruler or the sovereign. In every case, sovereignty is aligned with tran-

4. Were one to do a thorough study of the concept of "kingship," especially vis-à-vis medieval religion, he would consult the following materials: Per Beskow, *Rex Gloriae: The Kingship of Christ in the Early Church* (Stockholm: Almqvist & Wiksell, 1962); H. P. L'Orange, *Studies on the Iconography of Cosmic Kingship in the Ancient World* (Oslo: H. Aschehong and Company, 1953); K. F. Morrison, *The Two Kingdoms: Ecclesiology in Carolingian Political Thought* (Princeton: Princeton University Press, 1954); Ivan Engnell, *Studies in Divine Kingship in the Ancient Near East* (Oxford: Basil Blackwell, 1967); Erwin R. Goodenough, "Kingship in Early Israel," in *Journal of Biblical Literature* 49 (1929): 169–205; Goodenough, "The Political Philosophy of Hellenistic Kingship," in *Yale Classical Studies,* I (1928), pp. 51–103; and the comprehensive study of Francis Dvornik, *Early Christian and Byzantine Political Philosophy,* 2 vols. (Washington: Dumbarton Oaks Center for Byzantine Studies, 1966).

scendence from which it derives both content and status. Hence, the king is given place at the top of the vertical plane, a place assumed by emperor, pope, and preeminently by Jesus the Christ—*Christ Pantokrator,* or *Maiestas Domini* —whose representatives, kings, emperors, and popes are understood to be. In all such cases, divine kingship was able to combine the characteristics of sovereignty and transcendence.

Hence, because of its formalizing capacities, "kingship" can be employed as a motif by which to chart the occurrence and progress of vertical religion. When that religion is most fully developed, the kingship theme is most prominent. When that religion is full-blown, almost every social, legal, and theological tendency comes to focus on the figure of the king. For example, not until kingship was firmly established was there a structural position of unquestioned prominence for the pope. Concomitantly, not until the category of kingship was firmly entrenched was there the possibility for a fully developed *summa theologica.* Both receive their fullest development at approximately the same time. (And the two can do this together because, as Thomas declares, Aristotle's "prime mover" is also the *Lord*—the choice of the terms is significant—whom Christians worship.)

There is ample evidence to suggest that kingship may be the fundamental motif of medieval Christendom. It is the motif which is responsible for the development of papal claims, the motif most often called into operation when civil and ecclesiastical dominions come into conflict. And all of this is to be expected from the kind of schematism which is governed by vertical projection and equates sovereignty with the highest position. The category of kingship is a concomitant of vertical hierarchization. When one sees kingship theory invoked, he knows he is in the presence of what we have been calling Religion A. Indeed, kingship is the mode through which Religion A is most often effected. It provides for institutionalization. It insures a perpetuation of the institution in and across time. It gives the religion an authority structure which it needs to support both law and belief. Beyond all of this, kingship supplies piety with language. It places man in the throne room of God. It orients him *coram deo*. It makes faith something similar to willing obedience. Indeed, the entire sacramental-sacrificial structure depends upon *subjects* honoring God as *Lord*. And because the man so disposed is in the presence of sovereignty-transcendence, he is also in touch with the treasury of wisdom and the source of inner peace. In the throne room of God there is great calm. There is rest because there is no further place to which one must go: the king is the highest, surest representative of God on earth.

And, from other vantage points, the hierarchical grades between man and God which Religion A distinguishes can be transposed into levels of mystical ascent as well as social stratification. By means of vertical hierarchization, clergy are distinguished from laymen, celibacy is preferable to marriage (since the latter increases one's involvement in the world), the king rules but the people are ruled. In terms of ideology, the king gives the universe a center. His throne occupies the spot on which the entire universe focuses. From that spot the earth is renewed at the time of the great New Year festival. At that place, God too is present, more specifically than anywhere else.

Any scheme which runs horizontally rather than vertically, obviously, is going to be critical of Religion A's fundamental emphases. True to form, then, the exponents of Religion B—not least the theologians of hope—are often impelled to criticize the kingly, priestly, establishment religion. This tendency is also responsible for their appearance of being anti-clerical; it also gives them a kind of natural recourse to the common people (those almost forgotten in Religion A because of their lowly place vis-à-vis the position of sovereignty-transcendence). And it enables them to speak a simple language, simple because it lacks the many abstractions necessary to talk about the higher levels of vertical projection. For these reasons, Religion B directs its appeal to oppressed people (or, at least, it seeks to hold up oppression as a matter of grave concern): to those whom the kingly traditions have slighted, overlooked, forgotten, fundamentally maligned, or who have felt themselves totally dependent on the king's largesse. Religion B tends to grow up among those who do not live in king's houses or share the king's bounty. It is fostered by those who derive little benefit or comfort from kingly empires. And all of this Ludwig Feuerbach must have seen before recommending that Religion A's vertical plane be inverted.

It is somewhat of an irony, then—especially over against these sharp contrasts—that kingly religion (or the kingship motif itself) was promoted by the forward-tending, apocalyptic-immersed, horizontally ordered Religion B. In terms of the distinction we have been making, Religion A didn't simply supplant Religion B. Instead, it grew out of Religion B, by using the latter's ingredients. The kingship motif, which exists as a kind of formal concomitant to vertically ordered religious apprehension, was also spawned by the apocalyptic materials, the principal religious documents of Religion B. One can see this interlacing occur when he examines the content of religious art in the early Middle Ages. Much of the art which existed in the seventh and eighth centuries consists of biblical manuscript illuminations, most of which accompany the apocalyptic writings. The New Testament Apocalypse is a favorite source of manuscript illustration, but the Old Testament works—Daniel, Ezekiel, as well as the apocryphal writings—receive detailed attention as well. Hence, the art which exists is composed out of the rich panoplies of stories, images, and suggestions which belong to the apocalyptic mode. Much attention is given to such topics as Michael and his angels, the warfare between the children of light and the children of darkness, the radical separation between heaven and hell, the awfulness of the catastrophies which are reserved for the end times, and so forth. But, because the apocalyptic vision raises the question as to how it will happen that God's rule will in fact rule, as Moltmann rightly sees, and because it forces the question about the eminence of the kingdom of God (without which theme the apocalyptic mode would lose its very raison d'être), *the matter of divine kingship cannot be avoided.* Indeed, the kingship theme emerges as the central theme in the apocalyptic outlook. The king does not enjoy a "natural place" as he does when he is placed as mediator between God and man on the vertical plane; but the thrust of apocalyptic thinking rests eventually with the establishing of kingly rule.

Because of the way in which the kingship theme functions in both horizontally and vertically ordered religious aspiration—the first expecting the time when the king will in fact rule, and the second looking to the king as God's present representative on earth—the history of the two religions of Christianity becomes exceedingly complex. Horizontal religion, as the hope thinkers know, grows in situations of oppression; it belongs to people who have been overlooked, neglected, or forgotten by those who exercise sovereignty. It has not been the religion of the establishment; it has been given little attention in communities which understand that their own status is secured by a vertical hierarchy. But this is simply another way of saying that apocalyptic communities have understood themselves to be outside the mainstream of socio-political favor. As a result their hopes have been placed in possibilities whose realization requires an overcoming of the very socio-political regimes which are responsible for their exclusion from the mainstream. Because the existing socio-political matrix does not contain the facility for redressing the inequities registered against the oppressed people, such people come to expect a radical—and sometimes both violent and militant —upsetting of present order. Of course, such peoples have existed in all times, in many places, but always under oppression. Bloch's book *Das Prinzip Hoffnung* is filled with references to them; indeed, because of the way in which "hope thought" derives from the aspirations of apocalyptic communities, it can be referred to as an instance of "the religion of the oppressed." And, as Moltmann knows, a consistent history of Christianity can be told simply in terms of the aspirations of succession of such apocalyptic-minded oppressed peoples. Moltmann's chronicle consists of nothing more than a tracing of the way in which apocalyptic-oriented, oppressed-people Religion B was forced to go underground by the prevalence of establishment-oriented Religion A from the mid-third century A.D. until during, one must suspect, the current revolution. As short as Moltmann's sketch is, it nevertheless illustrates that Religion B feeds on its antagonism to the more prominent Religion A.

But, of course, the story of Christianity can also be told from the other point of view. Instead of being a history of so-called oppressed peoples, it can be "church history." This is by far the more typical way of telling that story. Most college and seminary courses in the history of Christianity, for example, are treatments of the history of the church; and the courses in the history of Christian thought treat erudite theology rather than the content of folk or apocalyptic religion. Such practices have prospered for so long that they come to be expected. Yet such practices imply a great partiality toward Religion A vis-à-vis Religion B.

But the story can also be told from both points of view, that is, from the perspective of the interweaving of the two religions of Christianity. While Religion A has certainly gotten the most attention through the years, this is probably due not so much to the great numbers of its adherents as it is to its facility for working itself into the socio-political matrix upon which attention has been focused. And while Religion B has been slighted through the years, this is probably due not so much to its sporadic existence as it is to its failure to claim anything but a position of ill repute upon the plane of vertical hierarchization. But, in point of fact, Religions A and B have coexisted within the Christian West from the first century A.D. until the present time. Coexisting they have been running in parallel fashion through the centuries, requiring each other both as contrast and for support. From time to time they swing far apart from each other; and at other times they even come to express mutual interests. At times the differences between the two religions are particularly manifest, as is true, for instance, in the present day. At other times, in the first Christian communities, for example, the differences between the two were hardly detectable. But the two strains have been active from the beginning. The differences between them are manifest in the conflicts between St. Francis of Assisi and those who did not understand him. They are implicit in Luther's *Address to the German Nobility* in which he called upon rulers, princes, and nobles to put an end to the peasants' revolt. And in modern times—to cite but random examples —the differences between the two religions are at least partially responsible for Alfred Loisy's quarrel with the encyclical *Providentissimus Deus* of Pope Leo XIII. To bring the matter up-to-date, it can be argued, I think, that the clash between theological positions which occurred during Vatican Council II can be attributed to the co-presence of the same two conceptual patterns. Such clashes are particularly evident in times of religious, cultural, social, and political upheaval—as, for example, in the era preceding the Reformation. But they must be just as real, although more subtly present, in times of relative calm.

In sum, then, the advent of a theology of hope in the mid-twentieth century signals the reawakening of a peculiar form of Christian consciousness to a large formative religious disposition. As we have noted, that disposition is thorough in its influence and massive in its scope. It possesses sufficient formative capacities to be able to sketch in a full and consistent religious orientation. On its formal side, it has both breadth and scope enough to stand as a veritable paradigmatic model of religious sensitivity. Hope theology, in short, derives from one of the two formative dispositions within the Christian religion. But, it does not follow from this that hope theology and the Christian religion are one and the same. They cannot be one and the same if the Christian religion has been formed by two contrary dispositions. It does follow, however, that hope theology can be fitted to an Augustinian perspective. This is not the perspective of the Augustine who ascribed supremacy to the *civitas dei* by placing *civitas terrena* in unfavorable contrast, but of the Augustine who also understood that the priority accorded to God does not violate the several senses in which "this world" owns intrinsic goodness and proper status. It was that Augustine who noted that the relationship between God and world is so complex that it can only be depicted by a simultaneous affirmation of contrary truths.

SEVEN

The Present, the Future, and the Transition

For I am convinced that God is not yet, and that we must
achieve him. Could there be a nobler, more admirable role,
and more worthy of our efforts?
                                        —Andre Gide

As indicated in its preface, this book works towards two
objectives simultaneously. It is first of all interested in providing an evaluative sketch of the range of interests which
are a part of the so-called school of hope. With this in mind,
it has undertaken its objective by cultivating a series of
approaches to the thought of the principal members of the
school, namely, Ernst Bloch, Jürgen Moltmann, and
Johannes Metz. The approaches it has fashioned are ones
which are calculated to penetrate the fundamental tendencies of each of these three constellations of philosophical,
theological, and religious affirmations. Secondly, the study
is designed to illustrate and support a proposal. Throughout
the book, reference is made to the formal characteristics of
hope philosophy and theology. From this vantage point, the
book is an exercise in approaching philosophical and theological thought in terms of form and structure rather than
by a simple computation of content. The book attempts to
cultivate a kind of morphology of conceptual schematizing.
It seeks to isolate and describe the formative characteristics
of the patterns of thought which Bloch, Moltmann, and Metz

employ in giving articulation to hope. As already stated, the book attempts to do both things at one and the same time.

Thus, the study has shown that the pattern of conceptualizing which all of the hope thinkers find operative can be characterized by horizontal projection. Each of the thinkers in the school fashions a perspective which depends upon a linear or horizontal model (which in turn bears certain characteristics in common with process philosophy, as this is usually understood). For each of the three thinkers, the horizontal model stands in contrast to models of conceptual arrangement which depend upon vertical projection. For all of them, that contrast is real, and is one to which attention is repeatedly called. Indeed, the contrast is so pervasive that many of the principal contentions of the hope thinkers turn out to be little more than horizontal as opposed to vertical renditions of Judeo-Christian religious affirmations. Consequently, when one tries to account for the novelty which is implicit in the hope school, he need not look much beyond the translation of affirmations from a vertical to a horizontal context. Some religious affirmations cannot be articulated vertically, just as all sorts of affirmations do not work horizontally. In pointing to these innovations, taking Bloch's cue, this study has found it useful to build upon distinctions between cathedral imagery (for vertical projection) and ship imagery (for horizontal projection). Indeed, it has expanded this distinction in order to argue that Christianity itself, and not only formal projection, is duo rather than singular. Within Christian history itself, these two patterns of articulation have existed side by side. And each has been responsible for developing a fullblown religious stance, one which can easily support a liturgy, a set of authoritative religious truths (be it doctrine or less), a pattern of prescribed social action, as well as the piety that is necessary to the formation of the religious life. Furthermore, each can depend upon biblical support. On the basis of those capacities, we have called attention to the existence of "the two religions of Christianity."

But there are other kinds of considerations which also come to mind which are of more than formal importance. Our inquiry need not be restricted to the hope school's morphology. It is one thing to be able to locate, describe, and penetrate the fundamental contentions of a certain group of thinkers. It is quite another thing to judge whether these contentions are really saying anything, and whether they can be supported. Thus, it is to a critical examination of the proposals of the primary figures in the hope school that attention will be directed in this chapter of the study.

There are three useful ways of assessing the promise of the hope school. It can be seen, first, as a viable current theological trend. Secondly, it can also be tested as a source of insights which are of religious benefit. And, finally, it can be looked to as an instrumentality for mediating the future. In the following paragraphs, these three testing foci will be taken in order.[1]

When judged on grounds of theological astuteness, the contentions of the hope school must be given an equivocal mark. It is both plus and minus, for the contentions are both edifying and disappointing. From the positive side, first, the mood is large, engaging, and expansive. It possesses the ability to draw upon the interests of artists, poets, designers, city planners, architectural historians, and people with other constructive talents in its discussion of the meaning of human life and the fulfillment of human destiny. Quite probably, however, the reverse is more truly the case: the

1. This chapter consists of an extension and elaboration of my remarks in the review article, "A Revolution in Theology," in *The Journal of Religion* 51, no. 1 (1971): 67–74.

theology of hope facilitates the entrée certain Christians covet with respect to deliberations about man's future which are occurring, formally and informally, in a host of other circles. It enables Christians to become party to those discussions, without having to abandon their own claims and without having to learn a totally different language. It knows how to make connections with the interest in the year 2000. It has talent for capitalizing on current millennial hopes. Furthermore, it is a theology which builds upon creative tendencies. It maximizes openness; it has freshness, and an unwillingness to yield to premature dogmatic closure. It likes the feel of dreaming dreams. It wants to enhance the vision of youth. It sees its own promise as being akin to the promise of youth. It regularizes the characteristic of being unfinished and of keeping the new perpetually alive. Consequently, it is able to juggle the content of the Christian faith, and to set it forth in new and somewhat different arrangement.

As noted, it builds on horizontal rather than vertical schematization. It selects time and change as norm over permanence, seeking for action rather than settling for theory. When it speaks of salvation, it does so in corporate-social, instead of individual-personal terms. When it looks for reality's basic stuff, it finds the same in historical events rather than in ontological dimensions. When it makes reference to time, it does so with a view to the future rather than giving predominant stress to either present or past. Instead of depending upon precedent in any traditional way, it wants truth to be disclosed through experimentation. Giving greater import to immanence than to transcendence, it also employs Heraclitus, rather than Parmenides, as its philosophical father. From start to finish it argues that human experience is more than an occasion for checking principles.

Life is to be lived. It cannot be deduced from a previously given and settled ideological scheme. Because of these large, all-sweeping shifts in theological orientation, the statements which men faithful to the Christian faith have found it necessary to say come out differently under the hope school's auspices. The shift implied is no mere tinkering with already established policy, nor a changing of certain key factors. Rather, it is thoroughgoing, an almost total change of emphasis. And change adds vitality—the kind of new life which comes from placing things on different maps, and then reversing the direction of the compass by which the map is ordered.

Therefore, the thinkers in the hope school can make theological assertions which cannot otherwise be made. At the same time, there is a host of statements which they cannot make, and vast ranges of human experience which they cannot hope to articulate.

Because what they say is usually said in contrast to what others have said, or to what was said in former times, their sayings are always dialectical. That is, most of the fundamental contentions are registered vis-à-vis their dialectical opposites: not theory but action, not the past but the future, not tradition but experimentation, and not "re" but "pro." The line of argumentation frequently takes the following form: "It is not this . . . but this." Consequently, there are losses as well as gains. When abstracted from their dialectical counterparts, the contentions of hope theology are often overstressed and one-sided. For example, the Christian faith can simply not be properly articulated by reference to one time tense exclusively. The "category" of hope can never gather together all that must also be said about faith and love. And apocalyptic awareness is not the only viable religious mode. Furthermore, the New Testament is not an "apocalyptic book" exclusively, and cathedrals are not necessarily antithetical to time. The analogies between cathedrals and ships are really much closer than Bloch lets on. And, with reference to the key distinction between up and down, a horizontal conceptual model also requires vertical projection, and a vertical conceptual model is not necessarily static. Such typifications work well on blackboard diagrams, but in fact—and in life—the situation is always much more subtle and complex.

The question arises, then, as to how serious the omissions of the hope school are, which is the other side of the question about the quality of its positive thrust. The answer given to the two-pronged question depends upon one's conception of the theological enterprise. If theology's schema are necessarily plural rather than singular, and if their purpose is to aid the religious man when he thinks and speaks, then the omissions may be no more serious than the gains are important. But, if theology is understood to be something more than the instrumentation which gives structure to speech, then neither the gains nor the losses can be construed in operational terms.

According to the position taken here, Christian theology is not Christianity, nor is it a substitute for or an adequate representation of the Christian religion. Theology is not the truth of the religion, for religious truth is not quite the same as theological truth. The hope thinkers employ a conceptual model which gives the Christian religious man a means of depicting things to himself, and may provide a portion of the religious community with the tools and images necessary to self-awareness. Thus, either the structural representation theology designs is helpful, because it is also fitting and resilient, or it is the kind of pattern which neither accurately depicts nor personally inspires. In this view, theology is a kind of detailed theoretical projection of a system of religious affirmations that can be sanctioned. Thus, hope theology cannot be judged to be absolutely true or absolutely false, for these are mistaken criteria. Rather, it is either vivid or not, consistent or not, principled or not, pointless or not, reliable or not, and most importantly, refreshing or not. It is refreshing if it gives and sustains life, and if its sustenance does not disappoint.

To talk of theology in this way is, of course, to admit the necessity for a plurality of theological perspectives. If there can be but one valid system of theology, a system which contains the sum and substance of Christian truth, then the hope stance is found wanting. Hope theology does not enable the Christian to affirm all that he feels compelled to affirm, nor can it begin to summarize scripture, tradition, or the cumulative mind of the church. It cannot be construed as the one normative theological system. It is normative only when it becomes a participant in a larger conversation; it is never in that conversation alone, but is dependent throughout on its vertical counterpart. Furthermore, there is no *one* normative theological system, not if Christian faith and vision perpetually transcend their own discursive representations. The theology of hope can be included among those several stances which have proven resourcefulness, but it need not be judged on the basis of its singular authority and eloquence. Such cautions or realistic assessments of its place are in keeping with the contention that there are at least two articulable religions of Christianity. If the religion is duo, theology must be multiple. In a multiple framework, the theology of hope can sound some brilliant notes within the concatenation of a much larger piece. But its effectiveness in that capacity does not imply that the theology of hope is that larger piece.

The same conclusions are reached when one tests the school for the religious benefits which it can assure. As has been indicated, hope theology can be understood as a source (or stimulus) of edifying, innovative insights. In this respect, it is understood by its fashioners to be necessary within Christian religious awareness. Both Moltmann and Metz call attention, for example, to the way in which a preoccupation with matters of "personal salvation" tends to cancel or mitigate the Christian's proper interest in caring for the world. When Johannes Metz talks about the need for "deprivatizing" salvation, he offers as his alternative a "creative militant eschatology." As these men view it, private religion is foreshortened in that it does not see the necessity of forming the ideal human community. Consequently, they both recommend that religion become "deprivatized," that its locus not be restricted to subjectivity and self-consciousness, and that its personality formation be construed according to the likeness of saints such as Thomas Münzer, Martin Luther King, Jr., rather than in terms of the monastic-mystical patterns of St. Benedict or St. Bernard of Clairvaux. Münzer, rather than Luther, Calvin, or even Erasmus, stands out as the most intriguing figure in the Reformation era. Thus, when the great men of faith are cited or enumerated, they turn out to be persons who serve very well as apocalyptic heroes. Were there a Judas Maccabeus in the Christian tradition, he would no doubt be called to mind frequently as a reminder of the form of action necessary to thwart the oppression which diaspora people feel. Judas Maccabeus belongs to Jewish rather than Christian history; consequently, nothing is made of him in Moltmann's and Metz's writings. But the situation they both portray is one in which a Maccabean figure could prove useful. For them, Odysseus would not be enough, nor even the odyssean wanderer who also exhibits the spirituality of a Dante. The current situation is so critical that it requires men (or a corporate man) of an active, revolutionary temper in whose creative socially redemptive work others can also find both inspiration and identity.

Here, too, one discovers religious strengths standing side by side with religious weaknesses. It is probably true that for many Christians, today and in earlier times, the religious life was sufficiently ministered to if its devotional, aspirational side was kept active. The theologians of hope have rightly observed that personal religious vitality does not automatically translate into active, responsible social involvement. The two do not stand together according to any cause-and-effect relationship, nor are they necessarily interdependent. Moltmann and Metz believe that social responsibility derives from a distinctive religious syndrome which must be cultivated on its own terms. Thus they also find it strategically necessary to pit the two dispositions against each other, at least in order to show that the two are distinct.

The shift from the one disposition to the other—the personal to the social, the private to the corporate—results in losses to the religious life as well as gains. The gains are evident. The losses are more subtle. The gains derive from active involvements; the losses register more in the ascetic religious dimension—the area marked by the disciplines of contemplation, meditation, and most important of all, perhaps, deep-seated, unquenchable personal peace. One can say, categorically, that the conceptual model in which a horizontal thrust dominates is not the apparatus which makes personal peace easy to come by. Instead of peace, or a sense of calm and equilibrium, the horizontal model bespeaks a feeling of restlessness. Instead of assuring that the storms have subsided and that one can abide in a place of rest, this theological stance gives expression to the kind of enervation which perpetually resists rest. For the hope stance, the forward thrust is ongoing, the context of operation is always restive, because time and change pervade all things. Because the world is in process, with man standing on the prior side of beginning ("whose genesis is still to come" in Ernst Bloch's words), rest must be regarded with suspicion until it is located beyond the continuum of crucial historical events. These events, in turn, seem to exhibit the characteristic of infinite extension. Within the horizontal frame, it is both naive and untoward to speak of peace where there is no peace. There is no sure ground on which to stand. But when the possibility of some immediate (even though fleeting and occasional) peace vanishes, so also does the affirmation that the world God made is good. Perhaps one can conclude from this, then, that the kind of serenity which certain trusted saints have exhibited in the past seems to articulate with their conception of the religious life in vertical rather than horizontal terms. Or, to make that judgment more substantive than formal, it may well be the case that hope is not the author of peace, that the peace which is tied to hope is almost projected beyond accessibility. After all, hope in a certain sense is its own reward; when the substance of hope has been assured, it is no longer hope but faith. And faith tends to run vertically even when it possesses horizontal extensionality. The Christian religion is duo rather than singular, and any depiction of it which plays upon only one of its two strains is bifurcated and, to that extent, impoverished.

But, at the same time, the theology of hope can be tested as a way of mediating the future. It argues powerfully that contemporary society is in a state of transition. It also properly understands that the transition (as Thomas F.

O'Dea remarks) is of an "epochal" kind;[2] that is, the transition is like that which occurs at the end of an age, or at that point in which one age gives way to the next. Moltmann and Bloch construe the transition in apocalyptic terms. It is seen within a drama of signalizing events which presage the dawning of the end, or, perhaps, the beginning. But even in nonapocalyptic terms, one can argue that the present transition is both real and profound. It implies not simply a turn to the future, but, at the same time, a colossal awakening of historical consciousness. Men have become aware that men have a history, and that history is something over which they have at least limited control. Similarly, with respect to the process of evolution, men have come to recognize that man's uniqueness seems to derive from his ability to engage the evolutionary processes, to be a contributor to the constitution of its designs.

The hope stance has successfully moved theology into the age of transition. It recognizes with a lot of men everywhere that environmental questions loom very large at the moment, indeed, so large that an awareness grows that a new age cannot be born unless such problems are resolved. (In this respect, the theology of hope articulates better with socio-political, than with ecological-environmental questions; but this is in keeping with Moltmann's observation that his theology links eschatology to history while Teilhard de Chardin, on the other hand, links eschatology to nature.) Moltmann's and Metz's theologies sense the importance of the transition, but they don't see very well that in an age of transition questions about the self emerge in an almost overwhelming way. In every age of transition—in the early

2. Thomas F. O'Dea, "Transformations of Thought in America," in *Thought* 46 (Autumn, 1971): 325–45, originally prepared for the meeting of the American Sociological Association, Washington, D.C., September, 1970.

classical Greek philosophical era, in the dawning of the Renaissance, the pre- and early Enlightenment period—the question "Who am I?" or "What is the self?" is forced upon mankind with unadorned, rudimentary force. Socrates asked it. Petrarch and Erasmus asked it. Immanuel Kant asked it. It is asked in every era of epochal change. Thus, while the strength of the hope position derives in large part from its recognition that it belongs to a transitional rather than to a stable period, its weaknesses derive in large part from its inability to raise the questions of the self in a correspondingly appropriate manner. Perhaps the fault lies in a basic inconsistency: it is impossible to square the stress on "deprivatization" (which is necessary to counteract the previous overstress on the personal factor in religious experience) with another stress on *self* (which is at the center of the questions raised by a recognition that an old order is passing away). And yet it is true that the question about the self surfaces when men lose confidence in their surroundings and begin to sense that life will never be the same.

This oversight, or conscious understress, on the part of Moltmann and Metz is probably responsible for the mixed response which hope theology has received since its inception in 1965. There is lively interest in its contentions regarding the resourcefulness of the future, but also a feeling that something is missing. In an earlier paragraph in this study, we referred to that missing element as a loss of the basis of personal serenity. Now that same structural weakness shows itself as an inability to touch or treat the problem surrounding the integrity of the self. And yet this may be more observation than criticism. In an age of transition, the question about the self emerges because that question is not answered. During times of relative stability—when the style of an age has become conscious—the question about the self does not occur, because, to a certain extent, it has already been answered. The reflective stances which develop during ages of transition cannot be expected to settle the questions about the self, then, for such settlements only indicate that the transition has already been effected. Perhaps the theology of hope should not be faulted for not resolving such questions of deep self-concern, but it must be criticized for not recognizing their appearance. In failing to note their occurrence, the hope theologians also fail to see their propriety in an age which they also claim to be addressing. Questions of this magnitude are not resolved simply by being pushed forward.

Similarly, cognizant of the transition that is being called for, the hope theologians have been unable to do much more than talk about it. It is as though a great gulf has been fixed: men, standing on one side, cast their aspirations to the other side, recognize that the goal is to get from here to there, then learn that they are without an instrument of passage. It is one thing to make observations about the ways in which Christians bring interpretive arrangement to their experiences and affirmations, and to make pronouncements about vertical and horizontal positionings. But it is something else to cultivate the delicate transference skills to facilitate that which is being recommended. It should not be assumed that performance will follow upon insight. It isn't that easy. Nor should one expect that the spirit of the religious life will immediately transfer when its raison d'être is moved to new ground, as though men can simply leave the old behind and embark on horizontal ventures. On the contrary, the magnitude and abruptness of the shift leads to personal and communal religious tensions of considerable complexity. For example, many of the components of whatever earlier religious life there was will not survive the transition; and the strategies required by the new set of circumstances are not to be possessed simply upon application. These observations hold true regardless of whether the transition is from orientations of permanence to orientations of change, or the reverse, or toward some innovative combination of the two. The methodological point must be obvious: instead of fixing sole attention on a future time tense, the hope thinkers must give greater care to the relation between present, future, and past, and the matrix which finds the three tenses of time to be interdependent.

But models also have influence on the formation of the religious personality. In this regard, one can expect that sustained interest in the future will create its own spiritual wastelands. One can reliably predict, for example, that concerted devotion to the aspirations of hope will be accompanied eventually by an increase in ascetical piety. This too is in keeping with the spirit of an age of transition, an age in which the question about the self is raised in overt, bold, and rudimentary form. When this occurs, it is appropriate for men (and not only for those with "Sunday influence") to exhibit an almost primitive interest in wanting to be religious. It is characteristic of men of such times to initiate deliberate religious strategies. Not only do they attempt to become more contemplative and meditative, but they also invite voluntary discipline. Nor are they at all shy about wanting to cut through whatever superficialities stand in the way of the uncovering and securing of their secret selves. Of course, apocalyptic communities tend to thrive on the ascetic temper. Thus, properly speaking, a theology of hope should be expected to share that mood. Yet, because it has not yet laid its stress on the dynamics of subjective religious life, this theology has not fully noticed the urgency and propriety of unencumbered, ascetical religious tendencies. But it must, and it will. However, the tension is a large one: a theology of the world, as Metz calls his version of the theology of hope, will be suspicious of attempts to revive strains of monasticism.

There are other senses, too, in which the theology of hope shows insufficiencies with respect to the transition it seeks to inspire. These pertain more to an attitude it fosters than to any substantial oversight. *The theology of hope is very, very sane.* Ordinarily, this would be reckoned as an unqualified virtue. Indeed, sanity should be judged that way especially when the subject is as sobering as the question of man's future. But conflicts arise when the future is treated sanely only, especially if this means that one approaches the future in the same way he thinks about everything else. This, of course, is not appropriate. The theology of hope acknowledges this, but the form in which it does so is not always in keeping with the acknowledgment. Futures are not made accessible by treatises on the future. They cannot be extrapolated from the past, nor peeled off the present. One's stand toward the future is not composed out of the same ingredients men use to react to other occurrences. And the solution is not to be found in theories about the reasons theories don't work. Men can only dimly envision that which is "still not yet." They can play with it. They can begin to work it out in their dreams. They can anticipate it, perhaps, in their actions and avowals. They can give it place in their role playing. They can bring their designs to bear upon it. But, in every case, their predilections will be principled by techniques very similar to flights of fancy.

A theology of hope that is truly future-oriented, and, at the same time, is willing to acknowledge that it is only a partial vision, would read very much like the best of science fiction—indeed, like some of the philosophical writings of

Ernst Bloch, particularly his *Traces*. But the present corpus of writings in the theology of hope does not read that way. Though its subject is apocalyptical and eschatological, its language is definitely not. It seldom gets beyond the second-orderedness it claims must be overcome. It does not display the agility it recommends. It does not exhibit the playfulness it talks about. It does not engage in the fantasy it says is necessary. It gives few hints of the dreamlike perception it cites as being anticipatory of the future. It speaks of being mobile and free as though these were qualities to which it is not yet ready to subject itself. Its glimpses are glimpses without reports, and its hunches go unrecorded. Thus, for all of its crispness and clarity and the ways in which it diminishes convolutions, the language used by Moltmann and Metz might just as well be the language used by Karl Barth and Karl Rahner. It is better suited to treat Barth's and Rahner's subjects than it is to engage in the pro-mythologizing and pro-constructing which ought to follow upon the hope school's proposals. Were the language in keeping with the program, one would expect the result to sound more like that of J. J. Tolkien, Sir Arthur Clarke, William Blake, Norman O. Brown, and Buckminster Fuller, or even the prolegomena to the New Testament Apocalypse. The literary mode is out of keeping with the affirmations that are being made. Instead of being theological discourse in the familiar, expected style, the product should resemble a display of kinetic art. The proposals themselves are in keeping with an apocalyptic mood, but the mood itself has not been engaged. The principal documents of the theology of hope are about apocalypticism, but they are not apocalyptical documents. Thus, Moltmann can talk about a carnival without being able to invite his readers to join him in celebrating its occurrence. The next time around, reparation is made: it is discovered that the play element is lacking, so, the oversight is acknowledged, and play is recommended too.

But is there any other recourse? No matter how well conceived, a theology cannot expect to be all things, nor can it pretend to satisfy every religious and conceptual demand. The theology of hope runs into its fundamental difficulty when it tries to do too much, that is, when it attempts to achieve two large objectives simultaneously. It tries to be a theology of hope, and it wants to be a systematic theology. In other words, it feels constrained first to create a theology of the future: a theology that will effectively draw man's attention to his religious responsibilities with respect to the future. In this lies its innovations. Then, secondly, it seeks to summarize the cardinal tenets of the Christian faith in a self-consistent manner. This is its systematic side. When the two objectives are combined, the product is a scheme in which "Christian hope" becomes the formative, fundamental motif, the basis of a new systematic theology. It wants to be a theology of hope, and it wants to be normative Christian theology. But instead of being a grand and worthy goal, this is really an overcomplication. One cannot have it both ways. There is a fundamental error in the assumption that a theology that draws man's attention to the future can use that perspective as the schema for setting forth a correct summary of Christian belief. If theology must always be normative, that is, if it must make biblical teaching and the articles of faith subject to a systematic principle, it really cannot be a theology of the future or a theology of hope. There is no reason at all why a theology of hope should not be conceived. There is no reason either why theologians should not attempt meaningful proposals about man's future. But, in each instance, the mode and form of presentation should be tailored to match the subject. A subject cannot be treated properly if every subject is treated in the same way. Nor are subjects properly conceived if they are seduced into being principles, categories, or components of systematic patterns of reflection. To follow the transition to the future is to leave behind the attempt at systematization. A theology of the future will not be normative or systematic. Neither hope nor the future has the schematic capacity to serve simultaneously as a systematic conceptual principle and as the formative sine qua non of Christian religious truth.

We are talking, of course, about literary styles and about the mechanics of innovative theological model building. And we are suggesting that the theology of hope really brings systematic theology beyond itself. It brings Christian theology beyond the ken of systematic principles. It is the case of a discipline in process of transcending itself, which, through that process, learns that it has been ushered into a setting which calls for innovative model building. Perhaps no self-respecting hope theologian is quite prepared for that to happen. But it seems that there is no convincing way to avoid it. In fact, there may be no reason at all to fear it. With reference to other disciplines which have grown to transcend themselves, and in specific commentary on Ernst Bloch, George Steiner has written:

> . . . wherever literary structure strives towards new potentialities, wherever the old categories are challenged by genuine compulsion, the writer will reach out to one of the other principal grammars of human perception—art, music, or more recently, mathematics.[3]

Perhaps the same will follow the inevitable transcending of typical theological conceptual structures. The point beyond

3. George Steiner, *Language and Silence*, "The Pythagorean Genre. A Conjecture in Honour of Ernst Bloch" (London: Faber and Faber, 1967), p. 112. This essay originally appeared in *Ernst Bloch zu Ehren*, ed. Siegfried Unseld (Frankfurt: Suhrkamp Verlag, 1965).

the old categories is not revised old categories, but, instead, another kind of grammar, not earlier theology updated, but a recognition of the propriety of other modes of awareness. In lieu of a systematic theology of the future, which is a contradiction in terms, there are really only mysteries—refreshing and terrifying—and able custodians or stewards of such mysteries. And, in addition, there is a compulsion to reach out toward other principal grammars of human perception so that religious avowals that elude systematic conceptual form can still be made. Only in this way can the theology of hope be properly grounded.

Should the fuller transition occur, men will probably come to look back upon the incidence of hope theology more as precipitant than accomplishment. Or, if the histories of theological developments in our time were written like architectural manuals, it might well be said of Jürgen Molt-mann, that, using Ernst Bloch's *Das Prinzip Hoffnung* as catalyst, he found a way of weaving traditional Christian themes around a renewed sense of man's hope by employing a model of horizontal conceptual construction. But, then, in the commentary, it would have to be added that it was generally recognized that the product of Moltmann's work really could not be likened to a cathedral. It was not cathedrallike in architectonic or structurally systematic senses, and it could not replace the cathedral in a variety of other religious and liturgical senses. Indeed, when referred to cathedrals, the theology of hope stands more as complement than as threat, more as friend than as enemy, and more as instrument than as surrogate. The designs of cathedrals and ships are close in important structural respects. Indeed, when seen according to the perspective of the long reaches of time, the cathedral is probably the fittest of instruments of passage.

But for now, not later on, it must also be said that the theology of hope has plumbed a line of religious resourcefulness to enable some people to affirm their own experience and to approach the world in positive terms. And this has come during a time when loss of confidence and loss of identity has reached epochal proportions. It has tried valiantly to keep men from losing heart in the world. And this has come during a time when a significant portion of mankind has understood itself to be a diaspora people, that is, a people not at home wherever it presently is. Somewhat ironically, then, the "yes" that men utter has not come from a belated recognition of the value of things now, but through a projection of their aspirations forward in time. And, probably most important of all, in certain key quarters of Christendom—places ravaged by war and cultural destruction—a recovery of hope signals that men are finding ways of coming to terms with their own pasts.

Based on an early assessment, this is the achievement of hope theology, but not its promise. Its promise lies in something else, namely, in the host of new potentialities it has set in motion but on which it yet has no sure hold. Yet, even in the recognition of the limitations of a perspective, there is profound and subtle achievement. For, when hope is alive, it is enough that promise be promise. Hope can indeed be valued for hope's sake. It can cherish dreams because there are such things. It can engage in fantasy because fantasy as fantasy is real. It can find the positive side of illusion, without feeling constrained to explain illusions away. It can become party to projection, for projection is also part of a constructivist's ploy. And, if the next moment in the progression of that élan is not a counter-theological position, but, music, art, liturgy, creative dance, yes, even mathematics, a theology of hope should be able to approach such delights as means of celebrating its own transcendence.

Bibliography

Bloch, Ernst. "Man and Music." *Mother Earth* (April, 1917): 56–60; (May, 1917): 85–89.

_____. "Man as Possibility." In *The Future of Hope,* edited by Walter H. Capps, pp. 50–67. Philadelphia: Fortress Press, 1970.

_____. *Man On His Own.* Translated by E. B. Ashton. New York: Herder and Herder, 1970.

_____. "Odysseus Did Not Die in Ithaca." In *Homer: A Collection of Critical Essays,* edited by George Steiner and Robert Fables, pp. 81–85. Englewood Cliffs: Prentice-Hall, 1962.

_____. *A Philosophy of the Future.* Translated by John Cumming. New York: Herder and Herder, 1970.

Braaten, Carl E. *The Future of God.* New York: Harper and Row, 1969.

Capps, Walter H. *The Future of Hope.* Philadelphia: Fortress Press, 1970.

_____. "A Revolution in Theology." *The Journal of Religion* 51, no. 1 (1971): 67–74.

Cox, Harvey. "Ernst Bloch and 'The Pull of the Future.'" In *New Theology No. 5,* edited by Martin E. Marty and Dean G. Peerman, pp. 191–203. New York: Macmillan Company, 1968.

Fiorenze, Francis P. "Dialectical Theology and Hope." *Heythrop Journal* 4, nos. 2–4 (1968).

Frei, Hans W. Review of *Theology of Hope,* by Jürgen Moltmann. *Union Seminary Quarterly Review* 23, no. 3 (1968): 267–72.

Green, Ronald M. "Ernst Bloch's Revision of Atheism." *The Journal of Religion* 49, no. 2 (1969): 128–35.

Hefner, Philip J. Review of Moltmann's work. *Una Sancta* 25, no. 3 (1968): 32–51.

Heinitz, Kenneth. "The Theology of Hope According to Ernst Bloch." *Dialog* 7, no. 7 (1968): 34–41.

Metz, Johannes B. "The Church and the World." In *The Word in History*, edited by T. Patrick Burke, pp. 69–85. New York: Sheed and Ward, 1966.

————. "Creative Hope." *Cross Currents* 17, no. 2 (1967): 171–79.

————. "God Before Us Instead of a Theological Argument." *Cross Currents* 18, no. 3 (1968): 296–306.

————. *Poverty of Spirit.* New York: Newman Press, 1969.

————. "The Responsibility of Hope." *Philosophy Today* 10, no. 4 (1966): 280–88.

————. *Theology of the World.* New York: Herder and Herder, 1969.

————. "Through Religion to Revolution." *Dialogue* 1, no. 1 (1968): 42–46 (published by Forum, Vienna).

Moltmann, Jürgen. *Hope and Planning.* London: SCM Press, 1971.

————. "Politics and the Practice of Hope." *The Christian Century*, March 11, 1970, pp. 288–91.

————. *Religion, Revolution, and the Future.* Translated by M. Douglas Meeks. New York: Charles Scribner's Sons, 1969.

————. *Theology of Hope.* Translated by James W. Leitch. New York: Harper and Row, 1967.

————. "The Theology of Hope Today." *The Critic* 26, no. 5 (1968): 18–23.

————. "Three Lectures on the Theology of Hope," translated by M. Douglas Meeks. *Kalamazoo College Review* 32, no. 3 (1970).

————, and Jürgen Weissbach. *Two Studies in the Theology of Bonhoeffer.* New York: Charles Scribner's Sons, 1967.

Muckenhirn, Maryellen, ed. *The Future as the Presence of Shared Hope.* New York: Sheed and Ward, 1968.

O'Collins, Gerald. *Man and His New Hopes.* New York: Herder and Herder, 1969.

————. "The Principle and Theology of Hope." *Scottish Journal of Theology* 21, no. 2 (1968): 129–44.

————. "Spes Quaerens Intellectum." *Interpretation* 22, no. 1 (1968): 36–52.

Das Prinzip Hoffnung. Review article in *Times Literary Supplement,* March 31, 1961, pp. 193–94.

Ruether, Rosemary. *The Radical Kingdom: The Western Experience of Messianic Hope*. New York: Harper and Row, 1970.

Rühle, Jürgen. "Ernst Bloch." *Survey*, no. 32 (1960): 85–93.

_____. "The Philosopher of Hope: Ernst Bloch." In *Revisionism: Essays on the History of Marxist Ideas,* edited by Leopold Labedz, pp. 166–78. New York: Frederick A. Praeger, 1962.

Schilling, S. Paul. "Ernst Bloch: Philosopher of the Not-Yet." *The Christian Century,* November 15, 1967.

_____. Review of *Theology of Hope. Interpretation* 22, no. 4 (1968): 480–83.

Steiner, George. *Language and Silence: "The Pythagorean Genre. A conjecture in honour of Ernst Bloch."* London: Pelican Books, 1969. Pp. 102–16.

"Theology of Hope, A Symposium." *Continuum* 7 (Winter, 1970).

Index